HELEN M. STEVENS'
EMBROIDERED ANIMALS

David and Charles

▲ *FIG 1*

The delightful harvest mouse is a perfect model: small, agile and able to adopt a myriad of pretty poses. His silky fur and quivering whiskers make him an embroiderer's favourite.

Title page: PLATE 1

'My Favourite'. This superb horse makes a wonderful subject for portraiture. Careful shading, use of contours and stitch variations capture both form and character. See Chapter 4 Best Friends, page 57.

5.5 x 7.5cm (2¼ x 3in)

Contents page: PLATE 2

'Bilko and his Mum'. Two loving cats, much loved by their owner, are embroidered in pure silk with the addition of real whiskers!

10.5 x 8.5cm (4 x 3½in)

For Diana, with love

A DAVID & CHARLES BOOK

David & Charles is a subsidiary of F+W (UK) Ltd.,
an F+W Publications Inc. company

First published in the UK in 2005

Distributed in North America
by F+W Publications, Inc.
4700 East Galbraith Road
Cincinnati, OH 45236
1-800-289-0963

A catalogue record for this book is available from the British Library

ISBN 07153 1803 9

Printed in China by SNP Leefung
for David & Charles
Brunel House   Newton Abbot   Devon

Executive editor   Cheryl Brown
Desk editor   Ame Verso
Project editor   Lin Clements
Art editor   Prudence Rogers
Book designer   Robin Whitecross
Photographer   Nigel Salmon

Visit our website at www.davidandcharles.co.uk

David & Charles books are available from all good bookshops; alternatively you can contact our Orderline on (0) 1626 334555 or write to us at FREEPOST EX2110, David & Charles Direct, Newton Abbot, Devon TQ12 4ZZ (no stamp required UK mainland).

CONTENTS

HELEN M.
STEVENS

INTRODUCTION

We have shared our world with animals since time immemorial. Indeed, before the planet was 'ours' it belonged entirely to the animals, and those of us who are fortunate enough to share our homes with pets or lodgers in the shape of bats and other wildlife know that life with four-footed companions can be a challenging but ultimately rewarding experience.

SUBJECT MATTER

Animal motifs are among the earliest recorded textile decorations. From distant, ancient Egypt and Aztec civilizations to the more familiar European-based Roman, Viking and Celtic design sources, animals share the embroiderers' world both symbolically and realistically: the pink bats of early dynastic Chinese textiles still fly in today's tourist souvenir embroideries and the woven horses of Viking ship burials are reincarnated in the myth and magic of current Tolkein-esque merchandise.

Interpretations, of course, change. The most primitive depictions of both bird and beast can, to our eyes, be a strange amalgam of naïve and almost modern stylization. Medieval embroideries contain some strikingly

◀ *PLATE 3*

Motifs from projects in each book of the Masterclass series create a lovely sampler of techniques. From top right, clockwise: common mallow (Malva sylvestris) *(Embroidered Flowers),* Camberwell beauty (Nymphalis antiopa) *(Embroidered Butterflies),* house sparrow (Passer domesticus) *(Embroidered Birds) and harvest mouse* (Micromys minutes) *(this book, Plate 10, page 17). From the simplest interpretation of* opus plumarium, *our primary filling technique (see Stitch Variations, page 92), on the flower to the more complex application on the mouse, a logical progression is achieved. In this book we shall recap on both elementary and more challenging uses of* opus plumarium. Embroidery shown actual size 19.5 x 20.5cm (7¾ x 8in)

lifelike images and, with the variety of materials and threads at the disposal of the modern embroiderer, the scope for lifelike portraiture is greater than ever before. Wherever we find our inspiration the subject matter is boundless.

In many of my books I have emphasized that subject matter, however daunting, should not be a curb to interpretation through embroidery. Anything that can be drawn, photographed, or otherwise captured in an artistic medium, can be recreated in embroidery – the parameters of the artwork might be different, but the result can be effective, emotionally charged and, above all, intimate. Ultimately, embroidery is a personal art form, which can capture, through silk, cotton and specialist threads, the spirit of the subject, be it a streetwise urban character such as a chipmunk (Plate 7, page 11), a cheeky garden visitor, a much beloved pet or the magnificent monarch of the vast, untamed wilderness (Plate 12, page 27).

In previous Masterclass books (*Helen M. Stevens' Embroidered Flowers, Embroidered Butterflies and Embroidered Birds,* D&C 2000, 2001 and 2003) we have explored the ways in which my 'signature' techniques have been used to interpret a variety of subjects. Examples are shown in Plate 3. In *Embroidered Animals* these techniques are taken a step further, giving life and personality to our closest companions.

INTERPRETATION

Most of us feel that we understand the anatomy of an animal. Unlike insects and birds that include essentially alien elements in their bodily make-up, such as wings, animals are reassuringly familiar. Generally speaking, they have four limbs, a body in the middle and a head – the tail may be something of a surprise to our human psyche, but it is an acceptable adjunct (Fig 2). There are, of course, exceptions to this rule, such as the duck-billed platypus (Plate 28, page 76) but this is an endearing eccentricity. Basically, we feel comfortable with animals.

What is extraordinary, however, is the sheer diversity of scale and dimension. We (and I include humans in the spectrum) are all warm

blooded, and yet our metabolisms are separated by phenomenal time scales. Gestation periods can range between days and years, body clocks between minutes and days. Whilst teaching embroidery techniques I have, jokingly, often described a bumblebee (Plate 4) as a small furry animal in a rugby jersey: in fact, the fiercely aggressive pygmy shrew (Plate 5) is only fractionally larger than the bumblebee. The difference is in its struggle to maintain warm-blooded life; it must kill and eat every hundred or so minutes just to survive. And we think we live in a cut and thrust environment!

Scale, therefore, is an all important element in the interpretation of design in animal embroidery. The size and application of stitches must be tailored to the subject matter, just as the choice of threads and their gauge is a skill to be learnt. In this book, interpretation of design and scale on differing backgrounds will be explored – the suggestion of deep under-growth or night-time activity on black, with its optional inclusion of spectacular effects in gold and silver thread, will be explained alongside alternative depictions on pale backgrounds.

As subject matter and its interpretation becomes more complex and challenging we will also look at 'rules that are there to be broken'. In a very few animal families the run of stitches flow towards unexpected 'cores'; fur and hair are also imitated in novel and innovative ways. What do horses and meerkats have in common? Wait and see!

WORKING THE MASTERCLASSES

As in my previous Masterclass books, the five projects given in detail take readers through a spectrum of techniques and interpretation – from the simple to the more challenging. Even if you have never worked these techniques before you will be able to follow the sequence from the familiar to the exotic, referring to the Stitch Variations section (page 92) for support. Materials (page 88) and Basic Techniques (page 90) will give you all the information you need to get started and, at the end of each project, present your work to its best advantage.

If you are a newcomer to this series, each Masterclass project may be followed in precise detail – full templates, colour charts and step-by-step descriptions of the work are included for every study. For readers who are

▲ *PLATE 4*

The white-tailed bumblebee (Bombus lucorum), *whilst not the largest of its species, finds welcome sustenance in early apple blossom. Though not warm blooded, the young queens need food to give them the strength to establish new colonies each spring. The lovely silky bodies of bumblebees always remind me of small furry animals. In the natural world, the hunt for food is, with mating, most creatures' preoccupation – one giving them the ability to pursue the other. The food chain is relentless: insect is preyed upon by bird and in turn is at the mercy of larger predators. Here, however, the robin* (Erithacus rubecula) *is unlikely to make a meal of its companion!*
10 x 11.5cm (4 x 4½in)

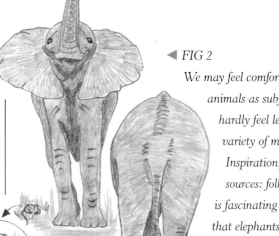

ready to step out on their own and interpret the designs more individually this book offers more scope than ever before to incorporate your own innovations. Suggestions are given as to how you might vary backgrounds, juxtapose elements to change the perspective of the piece or even merge elements of more than one project together.

Colour plates and line drawings throughout the book are designed to enhance and elaborate upon the Masterclass projects. Samplers can be worked to include elements of these illustrations (see Plate 3) and various tips and short cuts to creating your own file of motifs and designs are given in each chapter.

Whether you live in the town or the country, in a high-rise apartment or rural backwater, it is impossible to be unaware of the other species with whom we share our world. Thankfully, now, many governments have become conscious of the importance of maintaining a balance between our needs and those of our fellow inhabitants. But there is still much to be done. Every year dozens of species become extinct and publicity hovers on high-profile subjects: the tigers, rhinos, pandas . . . but smaller and no less important are the tiny creatures, marsupial mice (Plate 9, page 14), bats (Fig 20, page 77) and all the other hidden creatures existing on a knife-edge of survival as their habitats and lifestyles are threatened. This book will also explore these environments, from intimate nest site to territorial boundaries.

Early civilizations used animals as totems to represent their beliefs and act as couriers between mankind and the gods. By allowing even the smallest creature to disappear from our world we lose something of that camaraderie between this world and the next. We all have our favourites: cats, dogs, horses and the magnificent wild creatures that we are sometimes privileged to glimpse in the fastness of their own environments. As embroiderers we have an instinctive oneness with our world both past and present (I explored this in *The Myth and Magic of Embroidery* and *Helen M. Stevens' World of Embroidery*) and if the pictures in this book, and your own inspirational interpretations of the animal world, strengthen that link, we are only following an age-old precept.

◀ *FIG 2*

We may feel comfortable with the thought of animals as subject matter, but we can hardly feel less than awed by the sheer variety of models at our disposal. Inspiration, too, can come from many sources: folklore surrounding animals is fascinating – can it really be true that elephants are frightened of mice?

▼ *PLATE 5*

The pygmy shrew (Sorex minutus) is close to the limit at which a warm-blooded creature can exist and its life is one long round of predatory exploration. On tiny creatures the principles of stitching are similar to those on

larger animals, though the scale of stitches and gauge of threads must be chosen carefully to suit the subject. Something that never changes, however, is the highlight to the eye – a single white seed stitch suggests the 'boot-button' effect that conveys character.
6.5 x 7.5cm (2½ x 3in)

FUR AND WHISKERS

With a ripple of silky fur and a rustle in the taffeta of autumnal undergrowth, small animals demonstrate their mastery of camouflage. Blink and you miss it. Wait a while though, and a quivering whisker, fine as a gossamer filament, and a bright little eye might emerge once again.

When *On the Origin of Species by Means of Natural Selection* was first published in 1859, Charles Darwin laid before an intrigued and often hostile public a revolutionary concept of life on Earth. No longer was it to be assumed that every animal (mankind included) had remained unchanged and inviolate since the moment of its creation: rather, a thread of evolution could be traced, like Ariadne's silken route-map through the Minoan labyrinth, linking each species to its neighbour. Today, it might be hard to understand why such an idea was so scandalous – it seems obvious that each animal family is linked to the next by the invisible network of evolution, in itself no less miraculous than the Biblical creation story.

This interconnected relationship between species is a vital tool when it comes to interpreting the animal kingdom in any artistic medium. To capture successfully the nature of any creature it is necessary to have some understanding of its anatomy, and the logical flow of evolutionary changes from one species to the next can be helpful in the successful rendering of animal portraiture. This is particularly true in embroidery – through our unique medium we can express textures and tactile qualities more realistically than in any other. Capturing family likenesses and dissimilarities is a skill to be actively cultivated, and where better to begin than with the familiar and charming little creatures that often live closely alongside us?

◄ *PLATE 6*

In the commercial forests of eastern England the red squirrel is beginning to make a comeback. A thrilling flash of chestnut gold high in the trees is all most of us will glimpse, though in the autumn squirrels are seen more often at ground level (bottom right) as they hide nuts and acorns as a stash of winter food. A study such as this is obviously contrived – a montage of poses of the same creature – but it is still important to bear certain rules in mind. Keep scale accurate: the ragged robin (Lychnis flos-cuculi) and bindweed (Convolvulus arvensis), together with the transitory movement of the bee, link the other elements together.
Embroidery shown actual size
22 x 23cm (8¼ x 9in)

▲ *FIG 3*

Despite its name, the grey squirrel is far from
uniformly grey. Golds, browns and a variety of
buff greys combine to create its fur, which changes
throughout the year. This little study could easily
be traced off as a design (see Basic Techniques,
page 90) and embroidered mixing several shades
of fine silk in the needle at any one time (see the
design notes on page 20). The grizzled effect has
been created in the same way in Plate 8.

Darwin's interpretation of evolution depended largely on the theory of natural selection – stronger and more adaptable individuals or species were likely to supersede the less adaptable. In Britain, one of the most high-profile examples of this idea is to be found in the relationship between the red and grey squirrel. The squirrel family, *Sciuridae*, is one of the largest of the rodent groups, comprising not only the familiar tree-dwelling creatures, but also 'flying' and burrowing, ground-living members. The red squirrel *(Sciurus vulgaris)* (Plate 6) is Britain's native breed and was once to be found wherever there were broad areas of woodland. For 50 years from the mid-19th century onwards, the grey squirrel *(Sciurus carolinensis)* (Fig 3) was introduced from its original home in the hardwood forests of the eastern United States. Larger and more adaptable than its European cousin, it began to oust the red squirrel, without obvious signs of aggressive behaviour, by simply crowding it out of its habitat. The grey squirrel could survive anywhere – in small stands of trees, hedgerows, parks and gardens – and so it bred rapidly and successfully, finally infiltrating the red squirrel's essential territory of dense forest. The 'red retreat' became a rout and numbers are still declining, although now, at the eleventh hour, efforts are being made to reintroduce the red squirrel into 'grey-free' zones in carefully selected woodlands. In all fairness, grey squirrels are not entirely to blame for the situation as we must take responsibility for the decline in suitable woodland habitat and the rise in deforestation over the centuries.

The red squirrel is one of the most attractive and appealing of all Britain's native fauna. It has all of the features essential to create the 'Ahhh' factor in animal portraiture – cute characteristics, attractive colouring, bright eyes and a bushy tail! It is agile and can be captured in a variety of poses, as shown in Plate 6. From any of these we can begin to extrapolate the important elements of its, and most small animals', anatomy and also the techniques we need to employ to bring it to life in embroidery. But let's begin with a few simpler characters.

Walt Disney knew a thing or two about the
'Ahhh' factor: his young animals in particular
were often characterized in a certain way – eyes
were made larger and always dewily highlighted,
and surrounding features oversized to create
an image of vulnerability. Here, whilst not erring
too much towards to a cartoon effect, similar
tricks have been brought into play. 'Chip' is
cocooned by a rather large crocus and given an
anthropomorphic occupation – eating popcorn!
12 x 12cm (4¾ x 4¾in)

Whilst *opus plumarium* (literally 'feather work', see Stitch Variations, page 92) is more
obviously the technique of choice for bird portraiture, it is also the primary technique in
animal work. The sweep of stitches that give the technique its name, imitating the way that
feathers lie on a bird's body, are equally relevant to the flow of fur from nose to tail, each
strata of stitches describing the rippling of a muscle, the line of a limb or the pout of a
whiskered cheek pouch. Radial *opus plumarium* is always worked towards a central core.
The key is to find that core before we begin to stitch. This can be established at

▲ *FIG 4*

With Chip facing us (top), however many strata are needed to convey his markings, they must all fall towards his growing point, or core, at his nose. These directions are suggested by the arrows (below).

drawing-board stage. Whether you are working from your own sketches (always keep a notepad and a few crayons with you to make quick shorthand sketches that can be elaborated at the drawing board), or from a traced outline from a photograph or other pattern, think about the structure of your subject as you prepare your design. See Basic Techniques page 90 for how to prepare and transfer designs from sketch to fabric.

The central core of a subject need not be physically at the centre of a motif. Imagine a simple cartoon character – chipmunks come to mind. If 'Chip' (Fig 4 and Plate 7) is looking straight at us it is simple to establish the core of his being – it is his nose – and no matter how many strata of stitches we need to create his head and body, each would follow the next, flowing smoothly towards the core. Strata would merge seamlessly within a plane, or with the interruption of a voided line to separate one plane from the next. If Chip were suddenly to move, to look to his right or left, we would see him in profile and his core would move with him – the tip of his nose would still be the point towards which each stratum of stitches would flow. Look at the four squirrels in Plate 6: in each case, no matter what aspect of their bodies is presented to the viewer, the stitches all flow towards that essential core. Similarly in Plate 7, as Chip turns to the right, raises himself on to his hindlegs and picks up a piece of popcorn, we must still create a flow of stitches that imitate the behaviour of his lustrous fur.

If we think of the flow of stitches as a river flowing towards the sea we can bring other elements into the equation. Ears, front and back legs, a tail – all these features need to be linked into the overall movement. To incorporate these successfully we must create secondary cores towards which the stitches will initially make their way – like tributaries feeding into a greater river – before they are absorbed into the full sweep of strata (Fig 5).

The chipmunk (*Tamias striatus*), Chip, in Plate 7 presents the rather complicated challenge of blending his black, white and grey striped markings, shoulder and haunch into the overall flow of his coat. A simpler example of these techniques is shown in Plate 8, where two rabbits illustrate both full-face and profile portraiture. Like the cartoon in

Fig 4, the rabbit to the right is looking us straight in the eye. Each strata of stitches in his face flows smoothly towards his nose. A voided line suggests the break between head and body, the latter created by strata of stitches moving in succession toward the head. The voided line is then subdued to soften the break (see subdued voiding in Stitch Variations, page 94).

On the left-hand rabbit, we see the subject in profile. Two very subdued voided lines suggest the jawline and shoulder: all the other strata are uninterrupted in their flow towards the core. The ears of both rabbits are worked towards diffuse secondary cores, with subdued voiding again camouflaging the join.

▲ *FIG 5*

In a more complex subject such as this mouse, secondary cores are necessary, indicated by an asterisk at shoulder and haunch. Stitches should converge on these points, pivot and finally join the flow of the rest of the strata towards the main core at the nose.

◀ *PLATE 8*

Tolerated in much of Europe, the rabbit is persona non grata in Australia, having done much damage to the environment: even the Easter bunny has been replaced, on occasion, by the ecologically correct 'bilby', a native marsupial with conveniently long ears! The amorous proclivities of rabbits, however, have led them to have a place in most English hearts, even if only early in the year when spring and the heartsease (Viola tricolor) can turn a young man's fancies . . .
13.5 x 10.75cm (5¼ x 4¼in)

PLATE 9 ▶

*The Australian long-tailed
marsupial mouse is an amazing
little creature with a tail over
twice the length of its body –
I simply couldn't resist him!
Shown in this pose it is a
perfect example of 'full-frontal'
portraiture. Like Chip in Fig 4,
his nose is the obvious core of
the stitching. Subdued voiding
between muzzle and face, head
and body creates an effective
three-dimensional perspective,
and the whole outline is softened
by a very fine outer stratum of
stitching. The order of working
the face is set out in Fig 6.*
8.5 x 13.5cm (3¼ x 5¼in)

Rabbits were unknown in Britain until the 12th century when they were introduced from Europe as a valuable source of food and clothing. Many place names in England retain the word 'warren', proving their origins as rabbit farms in the Middle Ages. They were a profitable element in the rural economy for centuries, but in the last 200 years escapees have bred so profligately that rabbits have become a major problem in agricultural areas. Even so, who can resist the cuddly image of the Easter bunny and the much beloved childhood pet? Familiarity does not always breed contempt, and a domestic rabbit is a fine model on which to examine the flow of fur and the emergence of whiskers. A less familiar subject is the Australian long-tailed marsupial mouse (*Sminthopsis longicaudata*) (Plate 9) which nevertheless shares all the same features.

Facial features are as important in embroidered animal portraiture as they are in any medium of the human equivalent. The sparkle in an eye, the twitch of a whisker, the freckles on a muzzle, all create character and it is important to work vital elements in a certain order. It is always easier to work around an existing feature than to leave a vacant space and fill it later. Work eyes before the surrounding fur, usually at an angle to the later strata of *opus plumarium*, then work the nose and cheek pouches before progressing to the main filling technique. When all the surrounding features are complete, tiny studding stitches suggest the freckles from which whiskers may sprout – the whiskers worked in straight stitches overlying the base work (Fig 6).

The breeding population of the marsupial mouse is unknown, though it is thought to be rare. Hidden in the vast desert regions of central and Western Australia it retains its mystery. I have shown it with the mulla mulla flower (*Ptilotus exultatus*) for aesthetic rather than documentary effect as the fluffy oval heads of the flower complement the compact little body of the main subject: tail and stem balance effectively. Our first Masterclass project (Plate 10, page 17), though more authentic in choice of setting, uses the same design tool.

Meet Captain Courageous, a feisty little harvest mouse who has become a favourite in my classes as a perfect introductory model for animal work. The delightful bullet shape of the harvest mouse (*Micromys minutus*) makes him a relatively easy subject: whether in part profile (right) or full profile (left), clambering among the heads of corn in his natural habitat, his head and body require strata of stitches that flow almost seamlessly from rump to nose.

In the rough-and-tumble life of a harvest mouse the peak of the breeding season coincides with the traditional harvest festivities in Britain in August and September. Modern farming methods have brought the dates of the harvest forward but Captain Courageous is still to be found in his penthouse in the ripe cornfield.

▲ *FIG 6*

Voles are snub-nosed little creatures. Here, as in other studies, eyes are worked first in black (above), followed by radial opus plumarium *in several strata falling back towards the nose. Only after this ground work is laid should the white highlight in the eye and the freckles on the muzzle be worked in studding (see page 94), and the whiskers in long straight stitch (page 92).*

HARVEST MICE

Harvest mice, shown here slightly larger than life, are one of the smallest European mammals, hardly bending the ears of corn that supplement their diet in high summer. Agile, and with prehensile tails acting as fifth limbs to help with climbing and balance, their poses are perfect for our first foray into animal portraiture. Whiskers aquiver, Captain Courageous is on the case . . .

The embroidery is shown in Plate 10 (opposite) on a black background but could be worked equally effectively on a pale fabric (see cover illustration) and advice is given in steps 3 and 4 as to how this can be achieved. Whichever ground you choose, trace off and transfer the template design carefully (see Basic Techniques, page 90), making sure that all the details are included.

This study concentrates on the most important of the linear and filling techniques, stem stitch and *opus plumarium*, whilst also introducing simple and reflexing snake stitch. Easy decorative stitches (studding and straight stitch) give the subjects life and character with just a few darts of the needle.

TECHNIQUES

Refer to Stitch Variations, page 92 before you begin working if you are unsure of any of these stitches or techniques:

Radial *opus plumarium* • Directional *opus plumarium*
Snake stitch • Straight stitch • Voiding • Subdued voiding
Studding • Stem stitch • Surface couching

PLATE 10 ▶
Masterclass One: Embroidery shown actual size 21 x 21cm (8¼ x 8¼in)

Remember to pin your finished tracing firmly to your fabric before transferring the design. Do not pin through your carbon paper. Before completely removing the tracing take out one drawing pin and carefully lift the paper to make sure all the details have been transferred successfully.

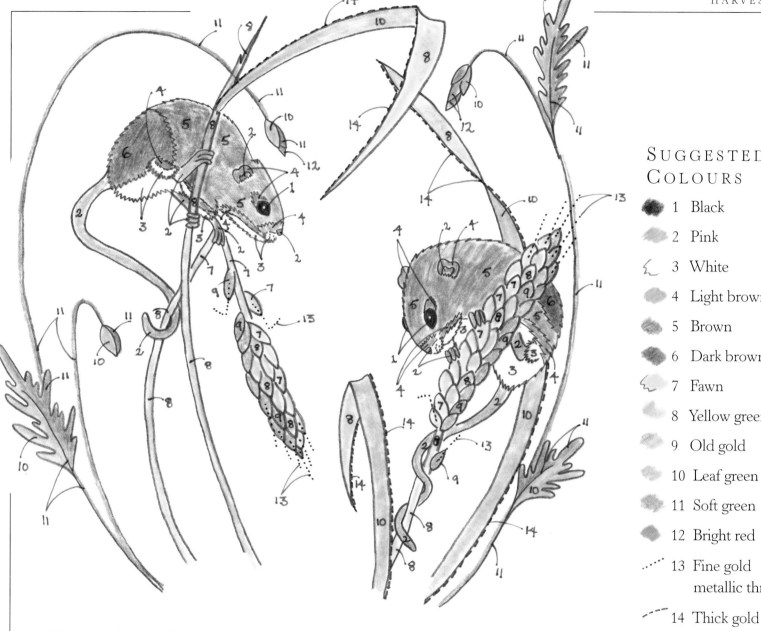

SUGGESTED COLOURS

1 Black
2 Pink
3 White
4 Light brown
5 Brown
6 Dark brown
7 Fawn
8 Yellow green
9 Old gold
10 Leaf green
11 Soft green
12 Bright red
13 Fine gold metallic thread
14 Thick gold metallic thread

Grey (not shown on chart, refer to picture details that follow)

Select your colours and threads using the chart as a guide, referring to the advice given in the Materials section (page 88). The colours shown on the chart are not representative of actual shades but are designed to make the chart simpler. Refer to Plate 10 to choose colours accurately – the shade names suggested in the list (right) should help. Where a large number of small fields abut, such as the individual grains on the ears of corn, only nominal fields have been annotated. Similarly, the fine metallic gold thread (13) is only shown selectively. Refer to the original embroidery for the full positioning of this colour.

DESIGN NOTES

A diversity of gauges and textures in your threads will really come into their own now (see Materials section).

Consecutively numbered stranded cottons make a good transition from one shade to the next but if you choose

to use a fine silk, strands of light and dark brown can be mixed in the needle to create an intermediate shade,

giving a gentler effect. Similarly, a variety of textures can create a more naturalistic contrast between

elements. Floss silk may be used for the fur of the mice, stranded cotton for noses, feet and tails.

Use the colour chart as a key to shading and make your own decisions as to thread texture.

The imagined light source in this study is immediately above the subject.

BEGIN WITH THE HARVEST MICE...

The order of working will apply equally to each mouse, regardless of which is illustrated at any stage.

1 Establish the core of the subject – the nose of each mouse – towards which will fall the main flow of the filling stitches. At right angles to this flow, work the eyes in black (1) in closely abutting straight stitches. Work a narrow triangular stratum of radial *opus plumarium* in pink (2) for the nose and small straight-stitched fields, also in pink, for the inner ears and the feet, broadening into snake stitch where necessary. Work the tail in simple or reflexing snake stitch in pink as appropriate. Begin the strata of radial *opus plumarium* for the fur in white (3) followed by light brown (4). If you are working in a fine thread, soften the abutting shades by working a few stitches with both white and light brown in your needle. Work the outer ears in light brown, each falling back to a diffuse secondary core.

2 Continue to build up strata of radial *opus plumarium* in brown (5). Work relatively short strata in the detailed areas around the face, lengthening the strata as you move back towards neck and body. Void around the eyes themselves but blend into the short strata of light brown behind them. In Plate 10 and the details shown, brown is created by mixing light and dark brown (6) in the needle to make an intermediate shade. If working on black, void carefully at each change of plane, e.g., between muzzle and cheek, jowl and chest and so on.

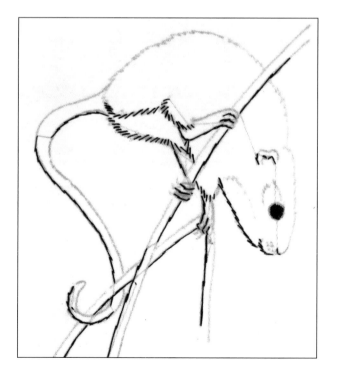

3 If you choose to work this design on a pale background, shadow line your subjects before going on to work the colours. Using smooth or fragmented shadow lining (see Stitch Variations, page 92), work fine black stitching on the underside of each element of the design. The left-hand mouse in Plate 10 is shown completed on a pale background in Plate 3, page 4. Be sure to hide the threads on the back of your work behind elements that will be covered with stitching on the front or otherwise these will show through the pale fabric.

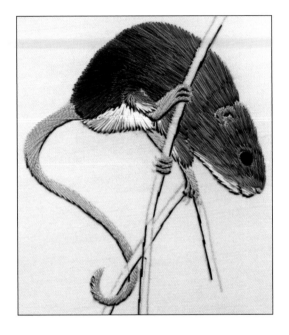

4 Regardless of whether you are working on a pale or black ground, complete the necessary strata of radial *opus plumarium* in light brown, brown and dark brown, smoothly blending one into the next. On the left-hand mouse, work a secondary core for the angle of the hindleg. If working on pale fabric, feed the extremities of the *opus plumarium* into the fragmented shadow line to effect a realistic furry outline.

MOVING ON TO THE EARS OF CORN...

Work short strata of radial *opus plumarium* to create lozenges (each falling back to its own hidden core) in fawn (7) and yellow green (8), voiding between each. Where feet clutch underlying features, overlay arcs of graduated stem stitch in grey to suggest claws at the end of each toe. These are too small to show on the chart – refer to the photographs.

5 Soften the outlines by subduing the voiding with fine stitches in whichever shade represents the nearer element of the design, shown here on the ear, cheek, rump and upper hindleg. Add the fine details of the eye highlight and muzzle freckles in studding in white and black respectively.

6 Complete the ears of corn by adding the final grains in lozenges of radial *opus plumarium* in old gold (9). Add whiskers to each grain in long straight stitches of fine metallic gold thread (13), right-angled if necessary. Work the stems of the corn in simple snake stitch in yellow green. Remember – always work your snake stitch *with* the curve of the motif.

7 Work the corn leaves in yellow green and leaf green (10) as appropriate in broad swathes of snake stitch. Surface couch thick metallic gold thread (14) where indicated on the chart. Work poppy stems in fine stem stitch in soft green (11). Work buds in radial *opus plumarium* lozenges of soft and leaf green for sepals, and bright red (12) for petals. Refer to Plate 10 for the poppy leaves, working central veins in soft green stem stitch with directional *opus plumarium* in soft and leaf green as appropriate on either side. See *Helen M. Stevens' Embroidered Flowers* for detailed studies of floral embroidery.

Finally, refer to the main photograph to work the whiskers in a very fine white thread in straight stitches. Allow these to overlay other features where necessary for a three-dimensional effect. Feel free to add other details of your own – see cover picture for ideas.

CHAPTER TWO

TOOTH AND CLAW

Deep in the dark green velvet of the jungle a patch of dappled sunlight and shadow appears to move with a life of its own. With the elegance exclusive to the cat family it resolves itself into the gold and black radiance of a tiger. Small creatures beware – the ultimate predator is on the move.

Whilst camouflage is an essential tool of survival for the vulnerable, it is equally effective for those whose business is to hunt. A tabby cat in the garden, in the tranquil shade of the herbaceous border, is all but invisible until it moves, and similarly for the tiger (Plate 11), the lion (Plate 12) and many other meat eaters: their fur is the very fabric of success – the cloak of invisibility.

The Bengal tiger (*Panthera tigris tigris*) is an awesome hunter, capable of overpowering a prey more than four times its own weight and though endangered (there are only around 4,000 left in the wild) is by far the most widespread of the tiger clan – once numbering eight subspecies there are now only five left. The Worldwide Fund for Nature together with the Indian government maintain more than 40 tiger reserves, and the survival of the tiger species as a whole may ultimately depend on saving the Bengal. They are poached for spurious traditional 'remedies' and, of course, for their glorious coat.

In the wild the tiger's fur, therefore, is both its blessing and its bane. The camouflage it offers allows the animal to catch its food: its beauty tempts the unscrupulous. Thankfully, we can enjoy the challenge and capture the glamour without fear of destruction or disruption! And what a challenge it is.

In Chapter One we explored the river-like progression of successive strata of radial *opus plumarium* flowing smoothly from nose to tail, shades merging, linear markings

◀ *PLATE 11*

'Tiger, tiger, burning bright in the forests of the night' wrote William Blake (1757–1827), his poetry capturing the 'fearful symmetry' of this glorious big cat. In fact, the tiger's markings are not entirely symmetrical and those of each individual are as unique and identifiable as fingerprints. Remember when working Dalmatian dog technique to stitch the 'spots' (in this case stripes) slightly larger than needed. The surrounding opus plumarium *will flood around them, stitched into each on all sides, making them smaller when complete. (See also Fig 16, page 58.) The fluffy stamens of the silk-cotton tree are harvested to make kapok, much beloved of soft-toy enthusiasts the world over. Here, a single strand of silk, topped with seed beads creates a stylized interpretation.*

Embroidery shown actual size
21.5 x 23.5cm (8½ x 9¼in)

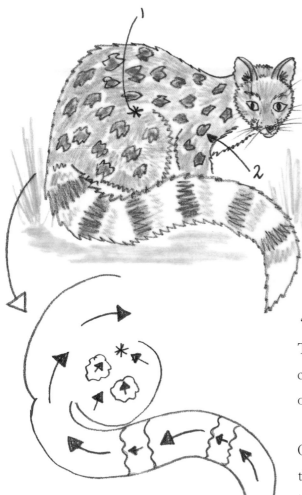

▲ FIG 7

The genet (Genetta genetta) *is a native of southern Europe and northern Africa and sports both spots and stripes. With a secondary core at 1 (*) and a diffuse core at around 2, Dalmatian dog spots, like the stripes of the tail, must be smoothly incorporated into the flow of the surrounding* opus plumarium. *The much simplified lower diagram shows the direction of working.*

moving with the overall flow of the stitches. With the tiger (Plate 11), that flow is continually interrupted by banded markings, and secondary cores are confused by their interaction. Initially, the key is to think of the stripes as spots. It might seem more natural to reserve Dalmatian dog technique (see Stitch Variations, page 94) for obviously spotted creatures such as the giraffe, jaguar or cheetah (Plate 21, page 56), but a spot is not always round – it can be any shape at all, as long as it is 'an area of one colour completely encompassed by another colour (or colours)'. It is the technique of choice for the tiger.

With the tiger, too, we meet the first of our (relatively rare) creatures whose primary core or growing point, is not precisely at the tip of its nose. All members of the cat family (and a few others who we shall meet as we go along) have a core at the 'stop' – the point just between the eyes where the forehead meets the bridge of the nose. Take a look at the family tabby, or examine a close-up photograph of one of the big cats – the fur changes direction at that point: downwards to the nose, then upwards and out to describe the rest of the face.

Work the facial features, eyes, nose and mouth, as we have already discussed in Chapter One, and then the markings: black bands – 'spots' with their stitches running in the direction of the strata to follow, similarly for face and body. The radial *opus plumarium* is then flooded around the spots following the usual rules of falling back to either the primary or secondary cores as appropriate (see Fig 7). Breaks (voids) between planes of stitches are softened by shooting stitches as necessary.

In Plate 11 a stylized setting is achieved by echoing Indian textiles. A characteristic element in Indian embroidery is the density of floral decoration, closely worked chain stitch designs, embellished perhaps with mirror (shisha) work (see *Helen M. Stevens' World of Embroidery*, D&C 2002). Here, I wanted to suggest the tiger in his natural jungle setting, whilst capturing the lively, naïve feel of a Bengali *kantha*. *Bombax ceiba*, the silk-cotton tree was too appropriate a subject to miss! Using simple directional and radial *opus plumarium* respectively, leaves and flowers are worked, the latter embellished with straight-stitched stamens and tiny seed beads. Stems and veins are added in surface couched metallic gold thread.

By contrast, the lion (*Panthera leo*) in Plate 12, unencumbered by style or setting is simply a portrait and an exercise in technical stitching. Readers of my generation will remember Clarence, television's cross-eyed lion of *Daktari* fame. Whilst not visually challenged, I wanted my lion to have that benevolent feel and so opted for the softest appropriate shades of gold and brown working throughout in a fine, single thread of silk. Again, the core or growing point is at the 'stop' and the short fur on the face is worked in strata falling back towards it. A different effect is required for the magnificent mane. A softly defined core is at the top of the head, where the mane flops to either side of the face. To that point flow successive courses of very fine, sometimes graduated, stem stitch, either singly or grouped into waves (see Fig 8).

Close-up work presents us with unexpected dilemmas. However fine a thread may be, it does not taper: threads cut from a long strand terminate abruptly, with the same thickness at their tip as at their base. For many years this frustrated me when working close-up portraits – then a solution presented itself, courtesy of my own cat. All animals shed their whiskers in the same way as the rest of their fur and a vigilant eye on the carpet can spot these treasures before they fall victim to the vacuum cleaner! The lion in Plate 12 sports real whiskers. Even if you do not have a pet of your own, most people are fascinated by the idea of their animals' whiskers being incorporated in a work of art, so ask friends to look out for prime examples – cat and dog whiskers are ideal – and build up a collection ready for your next project. Complete the portrait first, then insert a whisker (the tough end is quite sharp and will pass through your embroidery and fabric like a needle) at its desired point of origin, pull it through to the appropriate length and

▲ *PLATE 12*

When Aslan, the lion in C. S. Lewis' first Narnia novel The Lion, the Witch and the Wardrobe, *is shorn of his mane he is said to be 'only a great cat, after all', but, as the children soon discover, a lion is much more than that! A pride of lions has a unique social structure, the king of the beasts expecting his wives to feed him while he protects the pride's territory. A male lion can be tender with his own cubs, allowing them considerable liberties with his person but a shake of that magnificent mane and a warning roar can send them all scuttling back to Mum. We look at a wildcat cub in Chapter Three, Plate 19, page 46. 7.5 x 6.5cm (3 x 2½in) (whiskers extra!)*

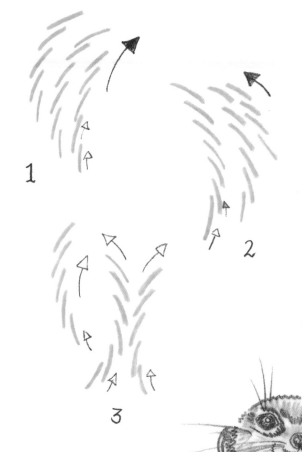

1

2

3

▲ FIG 8

*In this diagram orange represents
the stitches, white arrows indicate the
direction of individual lines of stem
stitch, while black arrows show the
overall flow of a group of lines worked
together to create a 'wave'. The two
techniques alternate randomly on the
lion's mane (Plate 12) to give a
naturalistic effect. 1 sweeps to the
right, 2 to the left and 3 shows a
scattered effect.*

couch in place. Snip off the excess at the back of your work. Apart from lending reality to your work it is an excellent conversation point!

The tawny-gold mane and coat of the lion is, of course, appropriate to its natural setting on the African plains. Sandy soil and parched grass, the dim shade of a solitary, scrubby tree and unrelenting sunlight call for a subdued, monotonal camouflage. The same holds true for the meerkats in Plate 13. Meerkats (*Suricata suricatta*) have become unexpected stars of stage and screen in the last decade thanks to Walt Disney's *The Lion King* and the BBC's brilliant wildlife documentaries. With a full-grown body length of only around 30cm (12in), they are small but tenacious and fearless hunters, tackling anything from scorpions to poisonous snakes many times their own size. Their colouring is more for protection than subterfuge as hunting is undertaken on a bully-boy basis: they surround and worry their prey until it is exhausted and falls victim to a fatal, clinging bite.

When not hunting, life revolves around the family group. Gregarious and playful, all members of the tribe are nevertheless responsible for the good of others: individuals are designated look-outs or nannies as appropriate. In the heat of the day they retreat to shade or burrows to wait out the worst of the sun. Long periods flat-out on the sand have given their fur a strange characteristic – a diffuse secondary core on the upper chest. Having worked their faces in the usual way, a hybrid radial/directional *opus plumarium* is needed to describe this grey, salt-and-pepper area (see Fig 9).

◀ FIG 9

*The dashed line down the middle of the meerkat's chest
indicates a diffuse core at which radial and directional
opus plumarium merge to give a 'hybrid' technique
that describes splayed fur. In Plate 13 the angle of
stitching is concentrated downward. After a long night
underground, one's fur becomes a little dishevelled!*

◀ *PLATE 13*

Meerkat young are privileged from birth – although Mum may go hunting all day soon after giving birth, returning in the evening to suckle the pups, they receive the undivided attention of a nanny during her absence. True creatures of the veldt, meerkats adapt to the extremes of cold and heat, emerging from their burrows in the early morning and absorbing the warmth of the rising sun to invigorate them, before shunning the worst of its midday heat. Their fine fur 'fluffs' out to capture the sunshine and I have suggested this by incorporating a few gold and black plied threads at the extremities of the opus plumarium *on each animal.*
17.25 x 19cm (6¾ x 7½in)

PLATE 14 ▶

The Ring of Bright Water *that gave Gavin Maxwell the title for his wonderful book about otters refers to the bubbles rising to the surface of the water – they are the first clue that an otter is swimming near. The sinuous shape of the otter and its prey create an S–Z pattern emphasized by the flow of stitches – a trick unique to embroidery! Similarly, the left to right flow of the current is subtly suggested by the floating embroidery: the long loose stitches are wafted across the fabric to create a feeling of movement. Natural static will maintain the position once the piece is framed.* 18.5 x 11.5cm (7¼ x 4½in)

The naturalistic setting in Plate 13 uses colours that reflect the main subject: sandy soil and rocks worked in a single strand of cotton, in horizontal or vertical straight stitch. Angled straight stitches suggest grass whilst stem stitch creates the basis of a scrappy thorn bush, tipped with chevron-stitched spines (see Stitch Variations, page 94). Meerkats are of the civet family; along a parallel branch of the predators' family tree we meet the otters – members of the *Mustelidae* group, the smallest of the hunters, including stoats and weasels (see Plate 26, page 72). They share the same air of fun, and the same prowess in the field.

From Tarka in Henry Williamson's classic nature story to Otter in Kenneth Grahame's *The Wind in the Willows*, these beautiful animals have been the embodiment of agility and athleticism. The Eurasian otter (*Lutra lutra*) (Plate 14) is agile on land but in the water becomes a master of his environment. Otters were once numerous throughout Britain and Europe, but man has been this beautiful creature's downfall. Hunting, for sport, fur or to protect fishing rights, has seen the otter dwindle to endangered status, and the use of pesticides, together with disturbance of the otter's natural habitat for water sports and industry have compounded the decline. Now, however, the otter's persecutor has in many places become its protector and 'otter havens' have been established to introduce captives back into the wild. This, and a ban on hunting, cleaner rivers and more sensitive farming methods may yet see otters back as a favourite, if rarely familiar, countryside companion.

Plate 14 returns to a relatively simple interpretation of nose to tail radial *opus plumarium*. The sweep of design and stitching is continued through the eel, snake stitched to suggest the sinuous, slippery nature of this otter's prey (Fig 10). The setting is reduced to a minimalist approach – straight horizontal stitches for a watery effect, enhanced by very fine surface couched silver thread worked in circles and randomly infilled with ice blue silk to create a bubble trail. Floating embroidery (see Stitch Variations, page 94) is an appropriate choice for waving fronds of waterweed.

An equally appropriate setting is chosen for this chapter's Masterclass (Plate 15): a red fox – with foxgloves! This is a fine young dog fox, alert and looking us straight in the eye, giving us the opportunity to practise frontal portraiture, together with broad sweeps of radial work flowing to central, diffuse and secondary cores.

Despite being another victim of man's love of hunting, the fox (*Vulpes vulpes*) is a modern success story. To see a country fox trot along a leafy lane at dusk, surrounded by wildflowers, its magnificent coat catching the last rays of the sunset, is one of life's treats. A less romantic though equally effective lifestyle has been adopted by many foxes – they have taken to urban living with enthusiasm. Suburban gardens, city backyards, alleyways and courtyards – all are now home to the versatile fox.

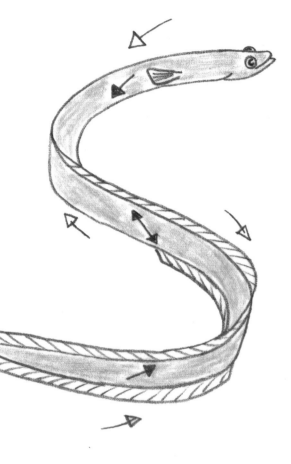

▲ *FIG 10*

However slippery a customer may be, snake stitch comes to the rescue (see Stitch Variations, page 93). With two sweeps of simple snake stitch (top and tail) and one of reflexing snake stitch (middle) an overall 'S' bend is achieved. The angle of stitching on the upper and lower fins is awkward as it must flow 'against' the curve to capture the texture of the fin. Try working from the tail towards the head for these sections.

FOX AND FOXGLOVES

The many story-tellers whose tales feature the cunning red fox, from Aesop to Uncle Remus, all agree upon one thing – he is as smart looking as he is sharp witted! With his dark mask and feet and splendid bushy tail, the red fox presents us with a series of textures from smooth to fluffy, all of which we can capture through adaptations of radial opus plumarium. *The foxgloves are a perfect foil.*

Whether working on a pale or dark background, trace off the template's details carefully and transfer them according to Basic Techniques page 90. Grasses at the base of the study are not shown on the template – add these freehand at the end of the project (advice is given in step 7). Remember to allow yourself plenty of extra fabric. A study such as this needs to be mounted and framed generously.

TECHNIQUES

Radial *opus plumarium* • Directional *opus plumarium*

Straight stitch • Stem stitch • Studding

Shooting stitch • Voiding • Subdued voiding

Broad areas of radial *opus plumarium* blend together here to create the fox's fine coat but the underlying body structure is also suggested straight stitched, fragmented shadow lines on the upper body indicate the contours of ribcage and lower back. They are subdued but nevertheless important details which add a realistic dimension to the broadest fields of stitching.

PLATE 15 ▶

Masterclass Two: Embroidery shown actual size 17 x 21.5cm (6¾ x 8½in)

HELEN M.
STEVENS

Everything shown on the template can be traced and transferred. Remember that if you work from a drawing not specifically prepared as a template to omit fine details such as whiskers – these, like the grasses, should be added freehand later. If you wish to add 'extras' to the design, do so at this stage – the moth from Masterclass Three, for instance could be added on a black ground, or a bumblebee on pale fabric.

SUGGESTED COLOURS

1 Black
2 Dark grey
3 White
4 Amber
5 Light ginger
6 Mid grey
7 Light grey
8 Mid ginger
9 Dark brown
10 Dark ginger
11 Very light green
12 Soft green
13 Leaf green
14 Deep pink
15 Mauve
16 Dark green
17 Light green

Carefully select your threads and colours. If working in very fine threads, one skein of light and one of dark ginger will allow you to mix a mid ginger thread, otherwise choose shades that progress subtly and smoothly from light to dark. Most stranded cottons and silks indicate these variations in shade by consecutive numbering. The annotation on the foxgloves is nominal – refer to the main photograph (Plate 15) for exact colour locations.

DESIGN NOTES

The imagined light source in this picture is placed in the top right-hand quadrant of the study.

If working on black fabric, omit the shadow line throughout.

BEGIN WITH THE FOX . . .

He is the focal point of this embroidery.

1 If working on the pale background, begin by shadow lining the whole of the subject in black (1). Differentiate between the smoother contours (lower cheek and inner ear) and the fluffier areas (upper cheek, muzzle, outer ear and so on) by using either smooth or fragmented shadow lining as appropriate. Work the nose, mouth and inner strata of the inside of each ear in dark grey (2) in radial *opus plumarium*. If you have a choice of threads, use a twisted, matt texture for these areas.

2 On either pale or dark background, begin to build up strata of *opus plumarium* following the colour chart: white (3) for the muzzle, black for facial markings and amber (4) to begin the upper face. Before reaching the eyes, complete their detail: straight-stitched irises in amber, overlaid with black to form the pupils, surrounded by strata of black to begin the mask. Delineate between the outer eye and the mask by working a very fine line of stem stitch in the void between the two.

3 Continue to build up the strata of the face, blending light ginger (5) into the white, black and amber as appropriate. Overlay studding stitches in black on the muzzle (whisker freckles) and in white on the nose and eye (highlights).

Moving on to the ears, work each in succession as follows:

Left: blend strata of amber into the dark grey and white into the amber in radial *opus plumarium*. In black directional *opus plumarium*, work the upper edge of the ear.

Right: Work shooting stitches in a fine white thread from the inner ear over all three strata. Soften the outer contours of the ear with straight shooting stitches at the same angle as the *opus plumarium*. Repeat this softening effect around the muzzle and rest of the face and head. Begin to work down the body in radial *opus plumarium* in light ginger (upper coat) and mid grey (6) and light grey (7) respectively for the chest.

4 Continue working down the chest and central body, blending light ginger into white and the extremities of the white into the fragmented shadow line. A diffuse secondary core originates at the top of the near front leg. Sweep successive strata of mid ginger (8), dark brown (9) and black towards the diffuse core. Work the far front leg similarly, in strata of mid ginger, mid grey, light grey, white, and dark brown. Continue to work down towards the feet in black, voiding between each toe (treat the area between each toe and foot as a small diffuse secondary core). Add the claws in small arcs of graduating stem stitch in dark grey.

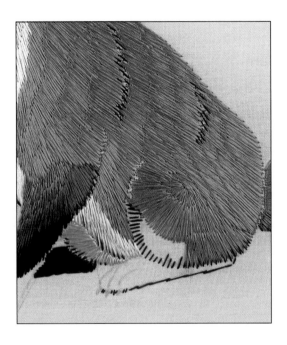

5 Continue down the back and belly in successive strata of light ginger, mid ginger, white and light grey. On the upper body work around and feed into the suggested contours of the ribcage and lower back.

Work the far upper hindleg in radial work in dark grey and then the far and near hindfeet in black, similarly to the forefeet. The secondary core of the near hindleg is indicated by the asterisk (*) on the template. Work radial *opus plumarium* in light and dark ginger towards the secondary core, sweeping around into the main flow of the stitches as you arrive at the rump.

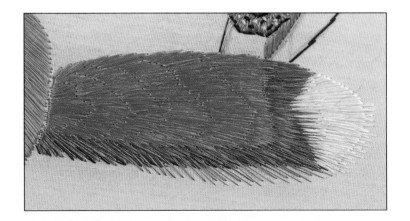

6 Working towards the rump, build up the fox's tail with successive strata of *radial plumarium* in light, mid and dark ginger (10). Tip the tail with white, and subdue the join between mid ginger and white with straight stitches at the angle of the underlying work in mid ginger. Now soften the outer contour of the tail, as shown below, right, with straight stitches feathering out beyond the main outline.

Referring to the main photograph (Plate 15), work your way over the whole of the fox, softening the outlines and subduing voiding to enhance the overall soft and furry effect.

MOVING ON TO THE FOXGLOVES ...

The right-hand frond of foxglove flowers is described and
illustrated below – work the left-hand frond similarly.

7 If working on a pale ground, shadow line the stems, flowers
and leaves in black. Referring to the colour chart, work the
stems and veins in stem stitch in very light green (11). Work the
leaves in directional *opus plumarium* in soft green (12) and leaf
green (13). Work the sepals in lozenges of radial *opus plumarium*
in soft and leaf green as appropriate.

Establishing the growing point of each bud and flower at the
base of the sepals of each bloom, work radial *opus plumarium* in
deep pink (14) or mauve (15) for the upper surface of each 'bell'.
Work the inner flower similarly in strata of dark grey and mauve
as shown, applying the opposite angle principle where necessary.
Overlay studding stitches in black and white.

Finally, referring to the main photograph as a guide (but using your own judgement), add
grasses and ground work in angled and horizontal straight stitching in dark green (16) and light
green (17). Work any additional features such as moths, butterflies or bees.

HELEN M.
STEVENS

MET BY MOONLIGHT

As dusk approaches, a rich black crêpe curtain falls, the scene changes and a new cast

of characters emerge from the wings whose natural home is in the shadow and half shadow

of the night. The moon is their companion; the stars their playfellows.

t night we can rely less upon our eyes and so our other senses become more acute. Walk out into an English country garden on a warm, balmy summer evening after the sun has gone down – preferably in bare feet. Touch is more sensitive: the cool grass between your toes, the brush of a moth against your face. Scents are more evocative and hearing more acute. What was that high-pitched squeak, a bat or a shrew? And the snuffling and rustling in the border . . . much more easily identified – a hedgehog searching for supper.

If our poor human senses are heightened by nightfall, the coming of darkness in the animal world is more like the lifting of a veil. For many creatures the hours of daylight are taken up in sleep and hiding. Only with the coming of the friendly protection of evening do they wake and make a move into the open. Hedgehogs (*Erinaceus europaeus*) (Plate 16) are one of Europe's most familiar night-time encounters – and the subject of much folklore. A favourite tale was that hedgehog 'familiars' would collect fruit, impaled upon their spines, and take it back to their mistress – the local wise woman or witch. If gullible peasants really saw such a phenomenon it was more likely that ripe berries attached themselves to the hedgehog during its foray into brambles and briars in search of prey: slugs, snails and beetles can find few hiding places when a determined hedgehog is hunting as its rigid spines allow access to the most inhospitable places, and protection against many predators.

◀ *PLATE 16*

From any perspective, the hedgehog is a charmer!
Hedgehogs can produce two litters in a year
in Britain, the first in early summer, shown here
with creeping cinquefoil (Potentilla reptens) *and*
lesser periwinkle (Vinca minor), *and a second*
in September. Young hedgehogs from the later
brood are less likely to survive, as a cold winter
can be too much for a less than well-insulated
youngster during its first hibernation. We can help
by putting out food (cat food is a favourite) in the
autumn, helping these later-generation babies
to build up a layer of fat.

The pretty roundel framework of flowers
is worked simply in radial and directional
opus plumarium *for flowers and leaves,*
with stem stitch and seed stitch for stems
and pollen masses.
Embroidery shown actual size
22 x 23cm (8½ x 9in)

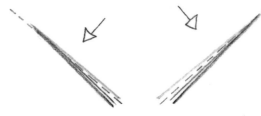

▲ FIG 11

A strong muscle, the orbicularis, lies just under the skin across the hedgehog's back and rump. As this constricts, the animal is curled into a ball and its spines radiate through 360 degrees. If the light falls from immediately above, a symmetrical division occurs. If not, or if the hedgehog is presented in a variety of positions, careful analysis of each prickle is necessary (see Plate 16).

A hedgehog's spines are created from the modified hairs that replace the fur from the top of its head to the base of its tail. They present a challenge in embroidery as their texture is significantly different to the normal pelage and yet is most effectively worked in the same thread as the rest of the animal. To solve this problem each spine must be treated individually (Fig 11). Depending on the animal's attitude and position, spines may appear at any angle (see Plate 16) and so the play of light and shade on every spine must be analysed and recreated. A black shadow line is first worked on the underside of each spine, followed by a long stitch in a dark grey shade. A lighter grey stitch is then angled to meet the first, creating a chevron stitch (see Stitch Variations, page 94) and finally a long white stitch is run through the whole arrangement, protruding at the tip to give a really 'prickly' feel to the chevron. If working on a black background the initial shadow line is, of course, omitted. The rest of the hedgehog's face and fur are worked according to the usual rules of radial *opus plumarium*: even if almost fully curled into a ball (centre, Plate 16) the core is gauged – his nose is hidden behind the prickles of his rump – and the stitches fall back accordingly.

Another little fellow who can form himself into a perfect ball, unfurling to emerge at dusk, is the common dormouse (*Muscardinus avellanarius*). As his name suggests, the dormouse was once common in Britain, now, however, rarely met by moonlight or at any other time. Hazelnuts are the dormouse's favourite food and evidence of a resident mouse are empty shells with neat, circular holes nibbled away to gain access to the nut. In Plate 17 a dormouse snoozes into the early evening, ready to wake when the sun goes down. Without prickles to complicate the matter, we can concentrate on the direction of the fur to create a successful portrait. Each area of the head and body must be analysed with regard to the juxtaposition of its neighbour. Whilst the nose is the obvious central core for stitching, and a secondary core is visible at the lower haunch, other cores such as the shoulder are hidden by a complicated attitude of the body. These must be estimated and worked towards, strata

The common dormouse's ability to sleep is legendary, as Lewis Carroll made clear in Alice in Wonderland, *when, at the Mad Hatter's tea party, the conversation took this turn:*
'You might just as well say,' added the Dormouse, who seemed to be talking in his sleep, 'that "I breathe when I sleep" is the same thing as "I sleep when I breathe"!'
'It is the same thing with you,' said the Hatter. . .
We shall be meeting the third guest at the tea party, the delightful Mad March Hare, in Masterclass Three.
11 x 8cm (4¼ x 3in)

of stitching 'disappearing' behind the nearer features. A pleasing continuity of both directional stitching and colour is effected by the choice of hazel leaves and nuts.

Just as at night the hedgehog gives away his presence by a loud snuffling, so the dormouse is in danger of attracting attention during the day by his breathing habits – dormice snore! A creature that seems to have no inhibitions whether awake or asleep is the racoon (*Procyon lotor*) (Plate 18). Originally natives of the warm forests of North America, racoons arrived in Europe in the 1930s, introduced by humans for the purposes of fur farming. The inventive racoon made short work of his confinement and soon escaped to begin successful colonies in the wild. Its extremely dexterous forefeet are

hand-like and can manipulate latches, lids and other man-made artefacts with ease and so its natural diet of fish, molluscs, fruit and grain is readily supplemented by the contents of dustbins, rubbish tips and, if resident humans are not careful, kitchens and larders.

I first met racoons during a trip to Canada. My reaction was to admire their dexterity – an emotion not shared by those who live with upturned trash cans and widely scattered litter – and I sketched the fellow in Plate 18 shinning over a chain-link fence as easily as over a natural hedgerow. A full moon caught and reflected the silver, cream and black of his

PLATE 18 ▶

Moonlight bandit! Whiskers a-tremble, this lad is up to no good! If you wish to emphasize certain features, such as those manipulative forepaws, try working in a different texture. Here, feet are worked in cotton, the rest of the fur in silk – the change in appearance is just enough to draw the eye to the element in question. Individual toes are worked in snake stitch (see Stitch Variations, page 93), merging into a broader band of stitching where they meet the wider area of the foot.
10.5 x 10.5cm (4 x 4in)

fine coat, while the black mask suggested his bandit-like personality. Don't be afraid to experiment with unlikely peripheral subject matter. A metal fence might, at first glance, not seem a promising setting, but worked in metallic silver thread, surface couched and, carefully interlinked, makes a striking change from the more usual foliate or floral framework. The moon, worked simply in horizontal straight stitching, is outlined in the same silver thread linking foreground to background, and the problem of where to end the fence is solved by applying randomly couched meandering woollen thread to suggest . . . anything your imagination can conjure. This is, after all, the witching hour.

Racoons do not occur in Britain but a creature with not dissimilar characteristics and colouring is the badger (*Meles meles*) (Fig 12). Though much more likely to be seen in a rural setting, badgers will enter gardens to take food left out for them if their confidence can be gained, and once at home they have been known to forage in waste bins and other receptacles. Whilst the rings on a racoon's tail are worked in successive strata of radial *opus plumarium*, the markings on a badger's head are more closely allied to those of the chipmunk in Plate 7 (page 11). Here, each stripe of colouring must be built up gradually, each stratum made up of alternative stripes and building at a uniform rate. These are suggested by the dashed lines in Fig 12.

Linear stripes (running nose to tail, such as on a chipmunk or badger) are always more difficult to capture than banded stripes (on the tiger, Plate 11, page 24). We need to tackle both, and in a variety of patterns, in a complicated subject such as the wild cat kitten (*Felis sylvestris*) in Plate 19. These cats, as their name suggests, are inhabitants of remote environments – the highland forests and moors of the far north of Britain – although they were once found throughout Britain and Europe (though not in Ireland). Persecuted remorselessly for generations, they almost disappeared in the 19th century but now, as we begin to have a better understanding of these beautiful animals, numbers are starting to recover and wild cats are once again slowly spreading south. Whilst adult wild cats might occasionally have taken a sickly lamb or perhaps a game bird, their reputation as ruthless and indiscriminate killers is undeserved. Rabbits, hares, small rodents and birds are their more usual prey – a similar diet to domestic cats turned feral. Indeed in some areas there is evidence that wild cats have mated with domestics, successfully rearing hybrid kittens that have gone on to boost the gene pool, which apparently reverts quickly to quasi-wild cat status.

In Plate 19 the basic shape of the kitten was worked first, incorporating linear and banded striping. Where colours abutted, the difference in shade was stark and this was softened by working over the whole area of the longer

▼ *FIG 12*

With the shorter facial strata of stitching suggested on this badger by the dashed lines, as the broader sweep of the body is approached strata can become longer, but remember to accommodate the secondary cores – their positions indicated here by asterisks.

PLATE 19 ▶

. . . talking of whiskers! As discussed on page 27 in
Chapter 2, if you are able to acquire real whiskers they
will give your animal studies a whole new perspective.
They must be surface couched into place very finely:
here the couching only occurs over other stitching –
on the blank fabric the whiskers lie free. He may look
angelic but wild cats are amongst the most difficult
animals to rear in captivity – those flattened ears give
the game away!

13 x 14cm (5 x 5½in) including whiskers!

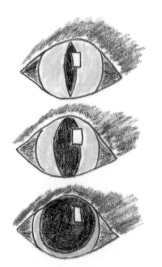

◀ *FIG 13*

Cats' pupils are upright ellipses; those of humans (and many other
mammals) are round, while some creatures such as grazing animals
are horizontal (see Balthazaar Plate 29, page 78).

The basic principle though remains the same: strong light – small;
dim light – large. The top three sketches show increasing pupil
size; below, the directional stitching needed to achieve the most
realistic description.

fur in straight shooting stitches, paler in the golden areas, and with the darker brown shade across the stripes. This softening effect was extended over the ears, and around the whole of the outline to create the 'fuzziness' so typical of the breed. An adult wild cats' eyes are a yellow-green chartreuse similar to many domestic cats' eyes. As with most young creatures they are blue in their early weeks, and in common with all cats, an ability to see in the dark goes with the territory!

In bright light the pupil in a cat's eye becomes a narrow, upright ellipse, allowing only a percentage of the light to reach the retina. As light diminishes, the pupil expands, until in the dark it becomes a large round pool of blackness absorbing every fraction of precious light and allowing the cat to see – really to interpret more accurately – the dim images around it. This sequence is set out in Fig 13. In embroidery, whilst the pupil is narrow, work both pupil and iris in upright stitching but as the pupil expands, the iris is more effectively worked in radial stitching to emphasize the roundness of both features (the direction of stitching is suggested at the bottom of Fig 13). Finally, highlight the eye with moonlight in two or three angled seed stitches in white, overlaying the groundwork.

If the moon is suggested reflected in the eyes of any animal, it must surely also be in those of the hare in Masterclass Three (Plate 20). Since before recorded history there has been a mystical link between the moon and the hare (see *The Myth and Magic of Embroidery*, D&C 1999). The man in the moon is a relative newcomer – the hare in the moon has been recognized by countless civilizations over the ages (Fig 14) and to see a Jack or Jill hare scamper across open fields by the light of a full moon is one of country living's most magical experiences.

On a warm summer night I glimpsed the scene that I have interpreted to create Masterclass Three. The moon was just rising, a great globe of apricot light, apparently suspended in gossamer strands of light and dark blue cloud. The Jill danced by, so light on her feet that she almost flew . . .

▲ *FIG 14*

Look at the moon carefully and compare it with this illustration (you may need to rotate the sketch slightly) and you will find the hare in the moon. Pagans believed that the fertility goddess Eostre laid an egg each spring, from which hatched her magic familiar, the hare (the origin of our own Easter Bunny!). It awaited its re-birth each year in the moon.

THE HARE AND THE MOON

In Aesop's fable the hare is overtaken by the tortoise because he is so sure of his sporting acumen

that he wastes time. The writer must have been familiar with the acrobatic antics of his subject –

for to watch a hare running is to recognize a supreme athlete at ease with its abilities. All four feet

off the ground at the same time, each bound is a long jump in its own right.

Masterclass Three is a deceptively simple design presenting us with a complex arrangement of radial stitching and secondary cores. Sharp voiding between planes, such as on the wonderful tangle of feet, contrasts with the softened voiding where body parts overlap – foreleg against breast and haunch against belly and rump. The three shades of brown are created by mixing colours in the needle.

TECHNIQUES

Radial *opus plumarium* • Voiding • Subdued voiding

Straight stitch • Seed stitch • Studding

Stem stitch • Graduated stem stitch

Dalmatian dog technique • Surface couching

With an obvious light source emanating from the moon, if working on a pale background the positioning of the shadow line is important. Unusually, the light is coming from below, so remember to shadow accordingly – detail 3 elaborates on this aspect of the study. This picture could be worked on a pale background with the moon transformed into a rising sun, in which case the moth could be omitted or be replaced by a distant bird.

PLATE 20 ▶

Masterclass Three: Embroidery shown actual size 23 x 18.5cm (9 x 7¼in)

Trace and transfer each asterisk to give the position of secondary cores and, if you
wish, refer to Plate 20 for a guide as to the direction of the radial work. At drawing board
stage you can add a few directional lines to assist in the final embroidery; simply sketch them on to
the template and transfer with the rest of the pattern, making sure they do not overlap the outline.

Use either consecutively numbered stranded cottons or silks for the graduation of light to dark or blend fine strands in your needle as discussed on page 20. If changing the study to a sunrise choose brighter colours for the sun and grass and replace the metallic silver with a similarly textured gold thread.

SUGGESTED COLOURS

1 Black

2 Light brown

3 Dark grey

4 Mid brown

5 Dark brown

6 Amber

7 White

8 Apricot

9 Light blue

10 Dark blue

11 Dull green

12 Pale grey

13 Metallic silver

14 Bright red

DESIGN NOTES

The imagined light source is with the full moon in the lower-right quadrant of the picture.

Smooth stitching is all important in this study. When working large areas in a single shade,

thread your needle with enough silk or cotton to work a substantial sweep of strata in one

operation. This will allow you to build up rhythm in your stitching.

BEGIN WITH THE HARE . . .

Pause before you begin stitching to familiarize yourself with the perspective of the creature –
which limb overlays which, and the positioning of various secondary cores.

1 If working on a pale background, shadow line carefully in black (1); if working on black pay attention to neat and uniform voiding. In radial *opus plumarium*, work the nose in light brown (2) and the cheek pouch in dark grey (3).

Work the iris of the eye in amber (6) in upright straight stitching and overlay black straight stitching at an opposing angle to create the pupil. Add a seed stitch in white (7) for the eye highlight.

Build up successive strata of light brown, dark grey, mid brown (4), black, amber and white as appropriate. Working towards diffuse secondary cores for the ears, build up strata of radial work in dark grey, light brown and black. If you have a change of textures at your disposal, work the inner ear in a more matt thread.

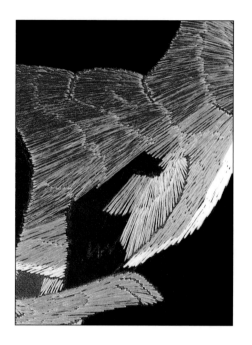

2 Moving down the body, continue to build up successive strata of radial *opus plumarium* over the neck (mid brown), upper back (dark brown, 5) and breast (amber and white) according to the colour chart. Begin working towards a secondary core at the shoulder (suggested by the asterisk on the template) in light and mid brown, smoothly sweeping strata around the pivot point. Continue stitching behind the foreleg and into the belly area maintaining the flow of work in amber and white from the breast.

3 As you reach the legs pay careful attention to the directional flow of your stitches. Analyse each section of the pattern carefully in order that you understand what is happening in each field to be filled. If working on pale fabric as shown here, work a fragmented shadow line for the shaggier areas of the outline and smooth stem stitch for the areas of shorter fur. Shadow lines should reflect the later addition of the *opus plumarium*, which should be able to engage with the shadow line when it reaches the outer strata of each section. On the hindlegs the 'ankles' are outlined in black (or left void on black fabric).

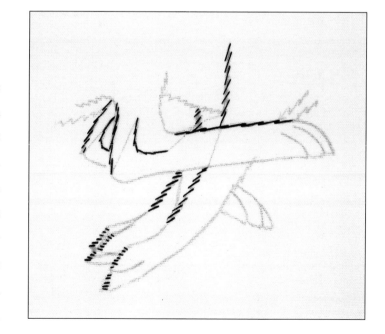

4 Bearing in mind the overall flow of stitches back to their respective secondary cores, work the forelegs and hindlegs in radial *opus plumarium* in light brown, voiding between planes as necessary. Continuing the strata towards the feet, working short accurate fields to create the toes. Add a claw to each toe in three graduated stem stitches in dark grey (see Plate 20).

5 Moving on to the secondary core on the haunch, work sweeping strata of radial *opus plumarium* in dark brown, mid brown and light brown to create the hip joint and rump, feeding the final strata into the upper hindleg stitches. The lower rump is then worked in a single stratum of radial work in white. Work the tail in two strata of radial stitching in black and white respectively.

Refer to the main photograph (Plate 20) and soften all appropriate voids with shooting stitches, always using the shade representing the nearer plane. Soften the lower outline similarly, and highlight the tips of the ears in white straight stitches. Add cheek pouch freckles in studding and whiskers in straight stitch.

MOVING ON TO THE MOON AND MOTH . . .

6 The moon and clouds are worked in straight stitching and surface couching. Fill the whole of the disc with horizontal stitching in apricot (8) and outline in metallic silver thread (13), surface couched. The extent of the clouds has not been suggested on the template – work these to your own design in a fine gauge of light blue (9) and dark blue (10), with horizontal straight stitches either abutting or overlapping the disc as desired.

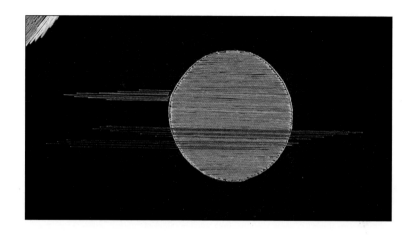

7 This moth is a Red Underwing (*Catocala nupta*). Work the three spots on the near forewing in dark grey Dalmatian dog technique, flooding pale grey (12) radial *opus plumarium* around them. Work the far forewing in pale grey radial stitching.

For the hindwing, work successive strata of radial *opus plumarium* in bright red (14) and black as appropriate. Segment the body by creating a series of small fields of straight stitching (slightly angled towards the rear) in pale grey, filling the voids between each with surface couched metallic silver, working two long straight stitches in the same thread (in a slightly narrower gauge if possible) for the antennae.

Finally, suggest the green field below. Again, this has not been outlined on the template but left to your own imagination. Work your stitches from left to right, abutting the horizontal straight stitching in dull green (11) up to the outline.

CHAPTER FOUR

BEST FRIENDS

Some childhood memories stay with us forever: the strange scratchy-soft wool of a lamb's fleece;

the silken, velvety muzzle of a favourite horse; the extra-blanket warmth of the family tabby curled

on your lap before the fire on a cold winter's evening. Animals are simply part of the family.

T he creatures we have lived with for centuries, cheek by jowl, are as varied as mankind's own civilizations. Prehistoric evidence suggests that dogs, cattle and horses were domesticated during or immediately after the hunter-gatherer period and, as lifestyles became more complex, so the variety of our four-footed comrades expanded. From those early days some animals have remained constant companions, others have changed their status; some from a source of food to pampered pet (who would once have conceived of a pot-bellied pig as a house-guest?) and some from work-mate to safari-park exhibit. The career of the cat has been amongst the most chequered.

The cult of the domestic cat in ancient Egypt has been well documented. The goddess Bast was their protector, and despite an appreciation of the cat's workmanlike abilities in pest control, it was also revered as a mystical beast. Perhaps this was why, in later ages and other lands, folk memory afforded the cat the dubious status of witch's familiar. Big cats, too, were part of everyday life: if their smaller relations could hunt, how much better to employ a lion or cheetah in the pursuit of big game? (see Plate 21 and Fig 15).

Plate 21 was designed as a companion to Plate 11 (page 24). Where the tiger is surrounded by elements of Indian extraction, the cheetah is set in a fantasy of Egyptian origin. The benevolent, stroking hands of the sun god Ra intermingle with the sacred

◀ *PLATE 21*

The magnificent cheetah (Acinonyx jubatus) *is possibly the least cat-like in appearance of all the big cats, though its hunting skills and lifestyle are typical. Famously, the cheetah is the fastest animal on Earth, reputedly achieving bursts of speed up to 112km/h (70mph). Its long tail acts as a balance and rudder during these phenomenal sprints. The surrounding decorative features are worked in silk and metallic threads. The outer whorls of the sun disc are couched in a very fine multitonal real gold thread, thickening into gold-coloured metallic thread towards the centre. Seed beads massed at the centre of the lotus flowers give a further dimension to the piece.*
Embroidery shown actual size
22 x 22.5cm (8½ x 8¾in)

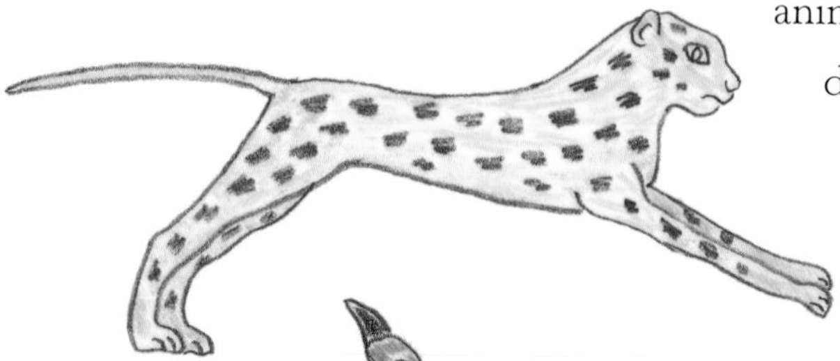

▶ *FIG 15*

Bast, or Bastet, the cat-headed goddess (top) was also a goddess of fertility, often shown carrying an ankh (as here) and a kitten. Cheetahs (middle) and lions were sometimes trained as hunting companions and the abilities of domestic cats (bottom) were obviously highly admired. All of these motifs are taken from ancient Egyptian wall paintings. When a family cat passed on, mourners shaved off their eyebrows to show respect.

▼ *FIG 16*

Many years ago when I was demonstrating the technique of incorporating one colour within a field of another, one of my students called out, 'I understand: you work a lot of black spots and then a white dog around them!' and so Dalmatian dog technique was born! Remember, though, that as your base colour floods around and into the spots, they will get smaller, as shown here.

lotus flowers of the Nile, while the cheetah himself is in a typical high-shouldered pose. The challenges presented by the tiger are repeated here with a few additions: the complexity of the coat pattern is greater and the slimline contours of the animal require extra attention by shadowing to describe the angularity of the subject.

As already discussed, Dalmatian dog technique (see page 94) should be worked within the rules of *opus plumarium* (in this case radial), the direction of the stitches within each spot determined by the later flow of the radial work. In Plate 21, the spots are very close together and the surrounding work is almost secondary to the pattern. The principle, however, remains the same and the execution can be made slightly easier by initially working the spots rather larger than necessary, so that in places they almost abut, giving a more apparently uninterrupted sweep of stitching. They are then separated by the *opus plumarium*, which feeds into each spot, decreasing it overall to a more appropriate size (Fig 16).

Worked on a pale fabric, shadow lining would help to emphasize the sharp outline of this elegant, streamlined big cat. On black, voiding can only do half the job, and to darken the gold of the fur too much would take away something of the drama of the piece. Here, then, I have overlaid dark grey in places to suggest such elements as the slimness of the flank and the contour of the ribcage. Never hesitate to try a new trick when it

Like the pretty floral roundel used in Plate 16 (page 40), the framing features here are simply worked in radial and directional opus plumarium, *stem stitch and seed stitch. They are repeated in miniature, drawing the eye into the main picture, where they are quite appropriate in a pastoral setting of meadow buttercup* (Ranunculus acris) *and ox-eye daisies* (Leucanthemum vulgare).

19.5 x 22cm (7½ x 8½in)

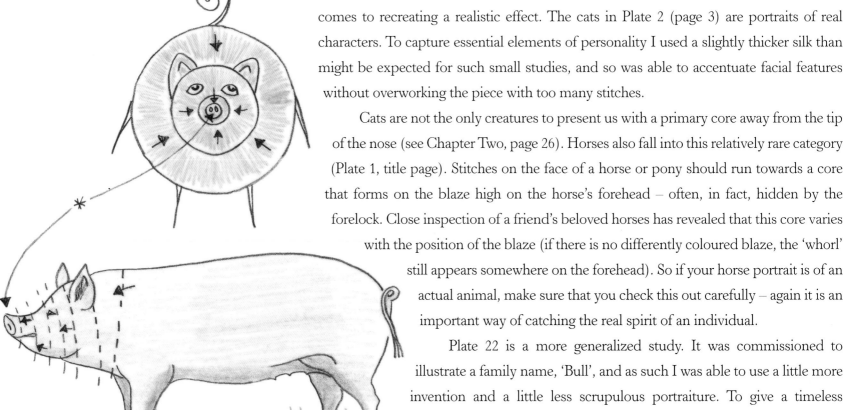

▲ FIG 17

The easy way of drawing a pig (top) gives a perfect example of where to find the core, and how all strata flow back towards it. Move the core to the side (bottom) and the strata follow, here on a more realistic sketch. Cotton strata (which would be used on a pig) should be of a similar size to silk, smaller to describe detailed features and broadening where less detail is required – as suggested by the dashed lines.

comes to recreating a realistic effect. The cats in Plate 2 (page 3) are portraits of real characters. To capture essential elements of personality I used a slightly thicker silk than might be expected for such small studies, and so was able to accentuate facial features without overworking the piece with too many stitches.

Cats are not the only creatures to present us with a primary core away from the tip of the nose (see Chapter Two, page 26). Horses also fall into this relatively rare category (Plate 1, title page). Stitches on the face of a horse or pony should run towards a core that forms on the blaze high on the horse's forehead – often, in fact, hidden by the forelock. Close inspection of a friend's beloved horses has revealed that this core varies with the position of the blaze (if there is no differently coloured blaze, the 'whorl' still appears somewhere on the forehead). So if your horse portrait is of an actual animal, make sure that you check this out carefully – again it is an important way of catching the real spirit of an individual.

Plate 22 is a more generalized study. It was commissioned to illustrate a family name, 'Bull', and as such I was able to use a little more invention and a little less scrupulous portraiture. To give a timeless element to the study I chose an 'old-fashioned' bull, a red-and-white longhorn. Here, texture becomes all important once again: the shine of silk would be inappropriate in this case, so a matt stranded cotton is chosen for the primary subject, the study lifted by silk in the framing features. In common with the cheetah, this substantial animal is largely defined by its stature – in this case four-square and sturdy – and shadow lining is used to emphasize the rump, haunch and ribcage. Where the bull is predominantly white, deeper shadows are suggested by pale and then darker grey forming an integral part of the *opus plumarium*, the flow of the stitches uninterrupted by the change of shade. Stitches fall back to the nasal core, the cotton blending from one radial stratum into the next, just as it would in silk (see also Fig 17). The simplest of landscapes offers an attractive setting, and the foreground framing features wildflowers appropriate to the imagined location.

It is one of the joys of embroidery that we can move from work on the grand scale to an intimate scene (Plate 23) without substantially altering our techniques. In this world of high-rise living for some, a much smaller animal companion is the only one appropriate and hamsters are a fine example. The golden hamster (*Mesocricetus auratus*) fills much the same niche for today's child as the dormouse did a century ago (Plate 17, page 43). Happy to be handled, lively and inquisitive, it can be a perfect pet where space is of the essence and two are even better than one! With animals as tame as these it is possible to get up-close and personal to a degree far beyond the normal human/animal contact and so we can really study the flow of fur to extend our understanding of the radial principal. When seen from the rear, the chubby rolls of fat and protective fur on the right-hand hamster's neck and upper back are suggested by

◀ PLATE 23
'The Conspirators': there is surely some mischief being hatched here! By positioning the highlight not quite central to the eye, an extra twinkle of reality is achieved. The imagined light source is, again, the key – put the highlight away from the shadowed quadrant of the study. As with all pets that live in cages long term, short bursts of freedom are important to keep up morale. Perhaps here the freedom is rather more extended than anticipated as our heroes have clearly made their way into the sweet pea bed.
11 x 15cm (4¼ x 6in)

▲ *PLATE 24*

This study of Benson was worked from a really good snapshot. If you intend to take a photograph as the basis for your embroidery try to find a non-fussy setting that will make tracing easier. Then, as you work the piece, remember that you are working (in this case) an embroidery of a dog, rather than an embroidery of a photograph of a dog. What 'works' in one medium does not necessarily give the same effect in another. Trust to your silk and your stitching to create depth and shadow.

9 x 10cm (3½ x 4in)

breaks in the stitching, which are left void and subsequently subdued and softened. This is just enough to give the roly-poly effect of his rotund little body. The same trick is used on the upper and lower back of the forward-facing character.

When two creatures are in close contact, such as shown in Plate 23, remember to analyse carefully which element overlaps which – this will give you the key as to which shade and direction of stitch is needed to soften voids. In this example the rump of the hamster to the right is in front of the belly of his companion – softening therefore effected in golden-brown worked at the angle of the rump. Above, the pouch and cheek of the left-hand hamster overlaps the upper back and neck of the other – the softening should therefore be worked in white and golden-brown respectively to bring these features to the fore. The whiskers, of course, serve to emphasize the point!

For those of us lucky enough to have the room, living with a larger animal adds dimensions to one's life that can only be imagined in an animal-free zone! Man's – or woman's – best friend has traditionally been the dog and it is still one of the most popular and widespread of pets. Meet Benson (Plate 24), a handsome young Boxer. This face is full of character, expression and personality, and it is a challenge to an artist in any medium. In embroidery we can use texture as well as accurate portraiture to achieve our goal. Working on a pale ground, shadow lining is essential. Once again, we must establish the core – this time at the nose, which itself is worked in straight perpendicular stitching in matt cotton. A couple of seed stitches in white silk give the luscious wet nose effect.

The complex arrangement of the slightly flattened muzzle, tight but slightly drooping jowls and 'worry lines' on the forehead are suggested by either shadow lining or voiding, and within that structure radial *opus plumarium* falls back towards the growing point, colours changing abruptly either with or across strata, as black gives way to tan or white. Eyes are emphasized by a fine outline in white and highlighted in seed stitch, whilst ears fall back to hidden, diffuse secondary cores. Finally, the smart blue collar is added in simple straight-stitched cotton, and the buckle in metallic silver thread. With a lad like this at your heels, 'walkies' can only ever be a pleasure. If a more relaxed scene is your style, maybe a cat is for you, though there is no reason why you should not have the best of both worlds – Tibbs and Tess (Plate 25) have been the best of friends for years.

In Masterclass Four we concentrate on true portraiture and the lessons explored here should give you confidence to approach studies of your own or friends' much-loved pets. Referring to the template (page 66) you will see that a firm, no-nonsense outline is important: don't try to include too many fussy touches but concentrate on essentials such as the exact position of markings. If you are not confident enough to draw your outline freehand, working from a good photograph is fine. Use a lightbox, if you have one, to trace off the outlines, or tape the photo and your tracing paper to a window and use the bright light from outside to throw the markings into relief. If you want to enlarge your study, make a tracing first and then enlarge it to the desired size with a photocopier, re-tracing before you transfer on to your fabric. If it helps, mark the site of an unusual core as an aide-memoire (Fig 18).

Tibbs and Tess are both black and white, with just a few touches of other colours to complete the effect. If your chosen subject is more intricately marked, choose colours carefully, but go for simplicity. Benson (Plate 24) has basic markings in black, white and tan. I have kept the choice of browns and tan down to around three, occasionally mixing colours in the needle, and allowed the sheen of the silk, emphasized by the direction of the stitches, to do the hard work of shading. On Tibbs and Tess, I have suggested only minimal grey shading in the white, allowing shadow lines, and the flow of stitches to have the desired effect. These two lovable rascals were just asking to be immortalized in silk!

▲ *FIG 18*

Remind yourself of where the central core falls at sketch or tracing stage and, if you wish, transfer it on to your fabric. Remember that any marks that are within the main frame of the animal will be ultimately covered with stitching, so if it helps to add the odd notation such as a reminder of the direction of radial work, go ahead.

TIBBS AND TESS

Two Masterclasses for the price of one – and everything down in black and white, what more could you ask for? Tibbs, of course, is that well-known breed the shorthaired cross, otherwise rather less respectfully called a 'Moggie', whilst Tess is a well-bred springer spaniel, but the two are inseparable and if one gets into mischief it is certain that the other is not far behind!

If you consider yourself to be wholly either a cat or a dog person, you can work either of these studies individually. If so, centre your chosen design on your tracing paper and, subsequently, on your fabric. You could use a smaller embroidery hoop for a single study, but if so, make sure that you still leave enough fabric around your outline to allow for ease of mounting and presentation.

It would be difficult to work this Masterclass, as it currently stands, on a black background, but you could change the fabric to a light pastel shade such as pale green, or a slightly darker neutral such as oatmeal. If you opt for a slightly textured ground, such as slub silk or pure linen, watch out for really substantial inconsistencies in the fabric and try to position the design so that primary outlines do not cross any imperfections.

> ## TECHNIQUES
>
> Straight stitch • Radial *opus plumarium*
> Directional *opus plumarium* • Seed stitch • Stem stitch
> Dalmatian dog technique • Graduated stem stitch
> Studding • Shooting stitch • Voiding
> Subdued voiding • Surface couching (optional)

PLATE 25 ▶

Masterclass Four: Embroidery shown actual size 17.5 x 18.5cm (6¾ x 7¼in)

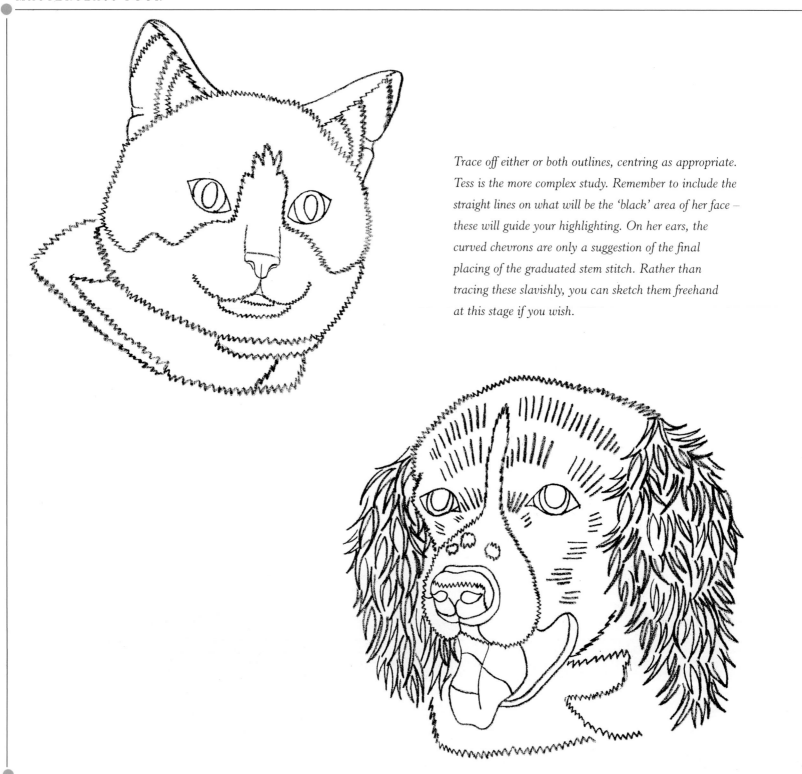

Trace off either or both outlines, centring as appropriate. Tess is the more complex study. Remember to include the straight lines on what will be the 'black' area of her face – these will guide your highlighting. On her ears, the curved chevrons are only a suggestion of the final placing of the graduated stem stitch. Rather than tracing these slavishly, you can sketch them freehand at this stage if you wish.

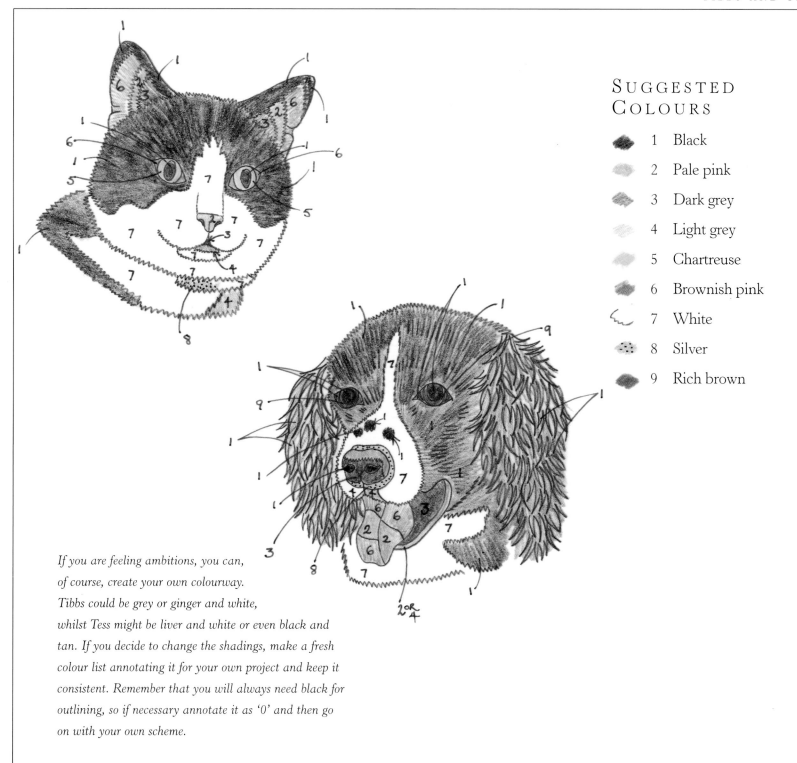

SUGGESTED COLOURS

	1	Black
	2	Pale pink
	3	Dark grey
	4	Light grey
	5	Chartreuse
	6	Brownish pink
	7	White
	8	Silver
	9	Rich brown

If you are feeling ambitious, you can,
of course, create your own colourway.
Tibbs could be grey or ginger and white,
whilst Tess might be liver and white or even black and
tan. If you decide to change the shadings, make a fresh
colour list annotating it for your own project and keep it
consistent. Remember that you will always need black for
outlining, so if necessary annotate it as '0' and then go
on with your own scheme.

DESIGN NOTES

The imagined light source in this design is placed immediately above the subjects. Remember that the

shadow line should be a suggestion rather than being set in stone. If you have changed your colourway

completely and are working on a black background, the shadow line should be omitted throughout.

If a variety of textures are available, use a matt thread such as stranded cotton for inner ears (Tibbs),

tongue (Tess) and nose and mouth (both), and floss silk for all other features.

BEGIN WITH TIBBS . . .

Cats always put themselves first – and Tibbs is no exception!

1 Carefully shadow line the fine features of the face and ears, using fragmented lines for the lower features, in black (1) and work the nose in upright straight stitch in pale pink (2). Add a couple of angled seed stitches below each nostril in brownish pink (6). Shadow line the eye in black and in upright straight stitching work the pupil in black and the iris in chartreuse (5). In slightly angled straight stitching work the inner and outer corners of the eye, towards their respective tips.

Work the inner ears in successive strata of radial *opus plumarium* in dark grey (3), pale pink, brownish pink and black, falling to hidden diffuse cores at the inner base of each ear.

2 Work straight shooting stitches (in a variety of gauges if you have them) in black and white (7) from the core of each ear over the underlying work to soften the inner ear. With the primary core between the eyes and secondary diffuse cores between the nose and upper lips, work successive strata of radial work in white, dark grey and light grey (4) to build up the inner facial markings. Work short, precise strata for the inner areas (in a finer gauge of thread if available). Broaden the strata and increase the gauge of the thread as you progress outwards. Now begin to add the black radial *opus plumarium*, together with a short directional band of stitching for each of the upper ears. Studding in light grey creates the freckles of the whisker pouch.

3 Continue to build up the white, black and silver (8) radial *opus plumarium* (shown in detail 2) to complete the markings on head neck and shoulder. Soften the outline between the upper and inner ear with black, in straight stitching and continue this softening effect between the head and ear and around the outline of the outer face. Treat the break between head and neck similarly. Add whiskers in long straight shooting stitches in white across the underlying work as indicated. Refer to Plate 25 for the positioning of the eye highlight, seed stitched in white, and add any optional real whiskers (see page 27) with delicate surface couching.

MOVING ON TO TESS . . .

4 Shadow line the lower features in black, fragmenting the line where necessary, and work the nose in upright straight stitching in light grey, dark grey and black. Highlight the wet nose with short, upright seed stitches in white (refer to Plate 25 for positioning).

Outline the eyes in black stem stitch, work the pupils in upright straight stitching in black and the irises similarly in rich brown (9). Work the corners of each eye in slightly angled straight stitching, towards each respective tip.

Complete the tongue and the inside of the mouth in directional *opus plumarium* in brownish pink, pale pink and dark grey, voiding at the ridge of the tongue and between the tongue and the inner mouth. Work the three Dalmatian dog spots on the muzzle in black.

5 Begin to build up the strata of radial work around the nose in light grey, silver and white, working in narrow strata for the delicate areas and gradually broadening the strata as you move outwards. Flood the white radial work around the Dalmatian dog spots. Work straight stitches in white to suggest the highlighted contours of the head.

6 Continue to build up the white, pale grey and silver strata, and then add the outer markings in black radial *opus plumarium*, allowing these markings to feed around the white straight stitches. If you find that the white straight stitches become too merged with all the surrounding black, then incorporate a few white shooting stitches into the black field of radial work.

Void between the upper muzzle and outer markings, and around the eye. When the outer markings are complete, begin to work the ear in arcs of graduated stem stitch in black (see also Fig 8, page 28). You may need more short arcs of graduated stem stitch than you have suggested in your tracing to fill the field successfully, so keep adding these freehand to the work until it is sufficiently dense.

7 Complete the basic form of the ear in black (upper ear), infilling any obvious gaps between arcs of stitching with appropriately angled straight stitches (lower ear).

Outline the eye in very fine stem stitch in white. Work the lower lip in a fine arc of directional stitching in pale pink or grey (choose which works best with your colourway) and feed the final facial stratum in black into it. Add a few straight shooting stitches in brownish pink to the inside of the mouth. Continue strata of black and white radial work down the neck and throat.

Finally, soften all appropriate contours, add studding in light grey for the whisker freckles and straight shooting stitches in your finest white thread for whiskers. Refer to the main photograph (Plate 25) for positioning of the white seed-stitched eye highlights.

CHAPTER FIVE

WEIRD AND WONDERFUL

Expect the unexpected fashion statement: a fur coat that miraculously changes from golden brown to snow-white in a few days, a couturier ensemble of coarse leather and the finest kid, angora in the farmyard. The animal kingdom is nothing if not eclectic in its choice of texture, tone and tactility.

Aeons of evolution have given mankind a false sense of our own superiority, but compared to the animal world we are amateurs in the field of survival. Some of the creatures that share our world today also shared it with the dinosaurs. Some can survive amid the filthiest of toxins and still thrive. Others, whilst rudimentary humans were cobbling together clothes from the skins of slaughtered bison, changed their summer and winter wardrobes with the ease of an experienced fashion model – and still do. The humble stoat (*Mustela erminea*) (Plate 26), a native of almost the whole of the northern hemisphere including the USA (and introduced into New Zealand), senses the coming of bitter weather and to maintain its camouflage in snowy conditions changes its fur colour from brown to white.

In Plate 26 I have tried to capture this astonishing little character in three guises: in winter (top); early summer (bottom right) and 'dancing' in the autumn (left). There is much folklore associated with the stoat. Able to kill prey over twice its size, it was once supposed that the stoat must resort to supernatural methods. This was apparently confirmed by their strange gambolling actions that mesmerized victims into a trance-like state. Thus immobilized, they fell prey to the stoat's darting attack, killed finally by a prolonged bite to the neck or throat. Any blood spilt would be lapped up by the predator, giving rise to the myth that stoats, vampire-like, sucked the blood of their victims.

◄ *PLATE 26*

In a delicate roundel tracery of seasonal subjects, the stoat is shown at his playful best. Baby stoats (or kits) are taken hunting by their parents and taught the tricks of the trade: dancing and stalking depending on their prey. This design invites the eye to travel around it by leading one feature into the next. Whilst the left-hand stoat is clearly fascinated by the spider, so, too, the right-hand character appears to have it in his sights. Above, the stoat in ermine is focused on his companion below. Although your design may be stylized, you can give it a realistic fillip by attention to the smallest details.

Embroidery shown actual size
24 x 24cm (9½ x 9½in)

▲ *PLATE 27*

Whilst tolerant of pollution, the three-spined
stickleback, like any fish, prefers clean water.
The fringed water lily (Nymphoides peltata),
given clean conditions, thrives in still or running
water, its strange, fringed petals reflected in the
diaphanous fronds of its root system. Continuing
the theme of delicacy, the fins, tail and prickles
of the fish are worked in a very fine silver thread
(one filament of a three-stranded thread), the
former two in angled straight stitch, the latter in
graduated stem stitch. See also Fig 19.
11.5 x 10cm (4½ x 4in)

In his winter guise the stoat is correctly called an ermine. Only the tip of his tail never changes colour, remaining coal-black. Royal and other aristocratic robes were once often made entirely of this black and white ermine – how many of these tiny creatures fell victim to such persecution is horrible to contemplate. It also became a heraldic term. How much better to study this jaunty character as a subject for embroidery?

Working on a pale background, and with a roundel framework of floral and foliate designs taking us (clockwise, from the left) from autumn, through winter and into the following summer, the stoat's year comes to life in Plate 26. Litters are born in spring and within ten weeks the young are independent. Adults then become more playful than ever, performing their 'dances' indiscriminately – here a large spider, an occasional tasty mouthful, is the unwitting audience. The principle of secondary and hidden cores forming the fulcrum points for radial stitching is applied in the same way as to the dormouse in Plate 17 (page 43). The study in ermine (top) shows the stoat in a more linear attitude. There is, of course, a secondary core at the haunch; otherwise all the strata flow smoothly towards the nose. The third pose, capturing the animal in early spring is a more traditional pose – here the interest is in the half-moulted coat pattern, where there is an abrupt termination between brown and white. Later in the year the golden brown colouring extends to all but the very lowest areas.

If the stoat's survival depends on hunting skills, for the three-spined stickleback (*Gasterosteus aculeatus*) (Plate 27) it is all to do with a tough constitution. Originally, this allowed the fish a choice of salt, brackish or freshwater: today its hardy characteristics allow it to thrive in waters sometimes too polluted for other fish – ditches, canals and even enclosed ponds. As an additional survival aid, sticklebacks are plated with 'armour' (here, three bony plates protect the fish's flank) and they are the only British freshwater fish to build nests and care for their young for the first few weeks of life. What a blueprint for success! An apparently complicated motif such as this can be built up easily by taking note of the order of working: this is set out in Fig 19.

By working an underlying strata of directional stitches, developing this into a scaly effect with 'laddering' (needleweaving through the existing stitches at right angles) and then overlaying the upper half of the body with a rank of straight stitches, a padded effect is achieved, giving a three-dimensional feel to the body of the fish. Surface couching gold and silver metallic thread around the outer edge of the body neatens the outline and suggests a slippery contour. Several of these tricks are useful touches in challenging underwater subjects.

Underwater studies, as we have already seen (Plate 27 and in Plate 14, page 30) can give great scope for imaginative touches. Bubbles, waterweed, an unexpected scattering of small aquatic beasts – all these can be fascinating adjuncts to a main subject, but when that main subject is as extraordinary as the duck-billed platypus (*Ornithorhynthus anatinus*) they pale into insignificance. When the 'duckie' was first discovered by Europeans in 1799 and a skin sent back to England from Australia, it seemed so improbable a creature that it was immediately declared a hoax. This is perhaps not so surprising, given that the animal had a bill like a duck, the fur of a mammal and feet with both claws and webs (differently arranged on fore and hindfeet).

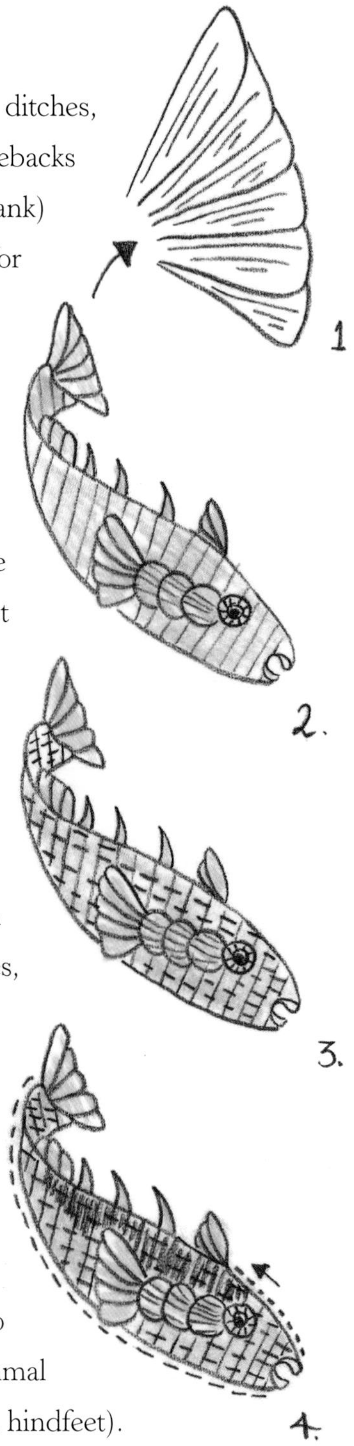

◀ *FIG 19*
Something fishy!
(1) The tail and other features are worked in fine metallic silver thread before the main body (see Plate 27).
(2) Work the body of the fish in straight stitching, angled across the subject.
(3) 'Ladder' or needleweave with a slightly contrasting thread. Pick up one or more threads, letting an equal number lie, and so on, following the contours of the body.
(4) Overlay a stratum of straight stitching on the upper body and outline the whole in silver or gold metallic thread in surface couching (indicated by the dashed line).

PLATE 28 ▶

Fossilized remains over 110 million years old prove that the duck-billed platypus has not changed since the time of the dinosaurs – a highly sophisticated and successful exercise in evolution. Though cautious of human interaction and so not often seen in the wild, its population is healthy and even spreading into the suburbs of Australian cities such as Melbourne. The freshwater shrimps are suggested by arcs of graduated stem stitch in gold, a 'blob' of a straight-stitched head and a plethora of fine legs and whiskers in white and metallic gold thread.

15 x 18cm (6 x 7in)

Later it was discovered that young were hatched from eggs and then went on to suckle their mother's milk and that adult males were poisonous, although they had no teeth to inflict a bite – the venom is held in a spur on the hindleg. Altogether the platypus must hold the title of the world's weirdest inhabitant. And yet he is a charming little beast!

On my first lecture tour to Australia I was determined to meet him, but they are shy in the wild and I eventually tracked him down in a marvellous wildlife park just outside Melbourne. Living in controlled conditions, with an underground glass wall allowing the public to see his antics, he nevertheless seemed unaware that he was the centre of attention – diving, pirouetting in the water and then dashing back up the bank and on to a favourite log to perform the ballet all over again. I was in love – and knew that an embroidery had to follow (Plate 28), but this was one of the hardest challenges I have ever taken on.

Design incorporating an unusual subject (to say the least!), texture, an impression of movement and buoyancy – and all within a limited colour scheme – put me to the test. I was, I thought, at least confident about the fur. This could be treated like the fur of any familiar animal, the radial *opus plumarium* needed to create sweeps and strata falling back towards the core. But where was that core? – somewhere beneath the rubbery plates that give way to the duck-like bill. After much trial and error, I eventually worked both bill and webs in a dull grey stranded cotton, padding slightly with underlying seed stitches beneath the bill, and then the radial work around them. I outlined the bill in silver metallic thread, couching it with fine silver-coloured silk, and added the wicked claws in a finer gauge of the same silver thread. Softening voids between the furry areas and letting them stand stark between fur and 'leather', then highlighting the primary contours of the feet with silver suddenly achieved the desired effect. My platypus came to life! It then only remained to add some freshwater shrimps ('yabbies'), bubbles and waterweed.

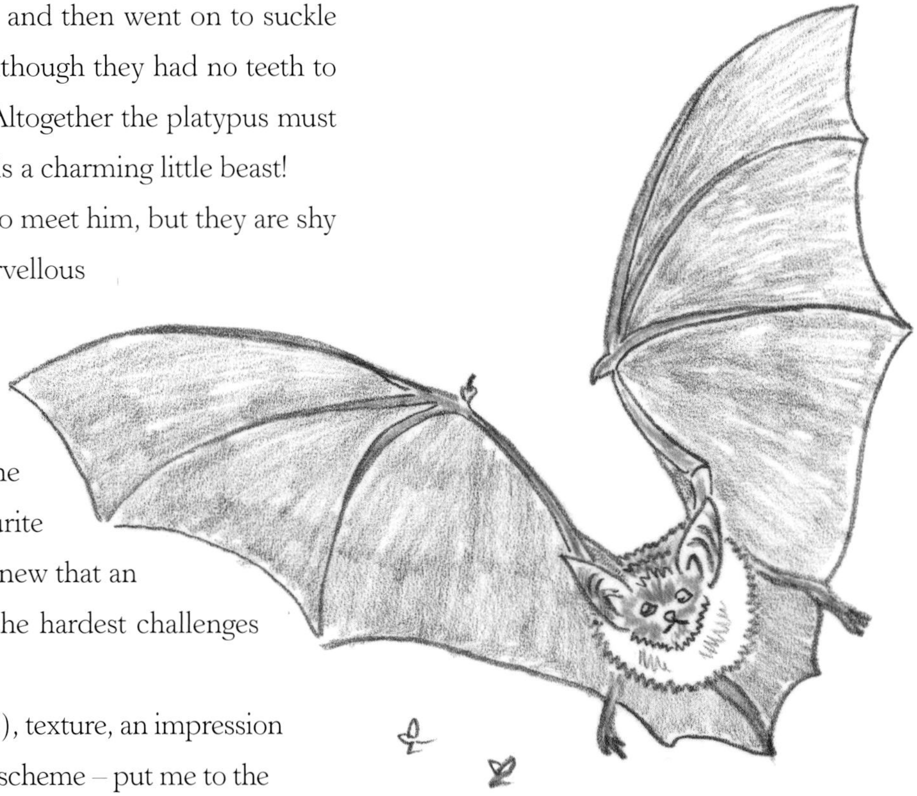

▲ FIG 20

Pipistrellus pipistrellus *is just one of a vast family: one in four of every animal species is a bat. Like little furry mice, the bodies should be embroidered in silk – but a matt thread such as stranded cotton would be ideal for the membrane that forms the wings.*

▲ PLATE 29

Like many grazing animals (sheep included) goats' eyes have a pupil formed by a horizontal ellipse. This is so that when they have their heads down feeding, they still have good forward and peripheral vision – a necessary precaution against wolves and other predators. Here, the ellipse is worked first, in black, the iris in a roundel of radial stitching and the highlight, as ever, seed stitched in white. Balthazaar's long eyelashes are then superimposed over the underlying work.

7 x 9cm (2¾ x 3½in)

Back in the UK, I began to see new textures with a fresh eye. The pipistrelle bats (Fig 20) that live in my attic and emerge on warm evenings to undertake amazing aerial acrobatics in the garden – the membrane between their elongated toes could be treated like the platypus' webs! I was on a roll and on the lookout for new subject matter. Soon, however, I was perplexed again: I met Balthazaar (Plate 29).

Balthazaar could have found a place either in this chapter or the last, as he is, indeed, a best friend of his human. Fifteen years old and with an alias of 'What-a-Mess', he was simply irresistible as a subject, but where to begin with all that silky coat, soft muzzle and hard, curved, grooved horns? Another session of analysis was called for. Balthazaar is an Angora goat. Originally natives of Turkey, they are now widely kept for their fleece which boasts fibres up to 20cm (8in) long and is spun into mohair yarn. Like the lion in Plate 12 (page 27) and Tess in Plate 25 (page 65) there is a contrast of texture between facial hair and longer coat, with a long muzzle halfway between horse and dog, floppy ears and contrastingly textured horns.

As ever, the best place to start is at the beginning. Clearly the core of Balthazaar's being is his nose. His cheeks, chin and muzzle are created by strata of stitching falling back towards a traditional growing point: only when we reach the beginning of his fleecy, longer hair do we need to change tactic. Here, I have shadow lined the most substantial of his kiss-curled locks to suggest their peculiar, almost ringletted nature. They are then worked in arcs of graduated stem stitch as in the earlier examples. Like Benson's ears (Plate 24, page 62), Balthazaar's fall back to hidden secondary cores, and I have worked his horns in successive strata of straight stitching, separated by voiding and lowlighted in places with fragmented shadow lines. The contrast between the stranded cotton used for the horns and the fine white and grey silk of his fleece works well. Having a variety of textures in your workbox will always stand you in good stead.

Continuing the theme of contrasting textural features, Masterclass Five (Plate 30) returns down under. Like the platypus, the koala (*Phascolarctos cinereus*) is an icon of Australia – its apparently idyllic, laid-back lifestyle seems typical of that great country's approach to most things – but it's all part of the koala's survival strategy. Eucalypt leaves are its exclusive diet: hard to digest and nutrient-poor. To thrive under these conditions the koala simply goes to sleep and conserves energy: watch one for a while, engaged in virtually any activity and you will see it just doze off mid-action. Hopefully, you will find Masterclass Five a relaxing project. It incorporates all the lessons we have learnt, bringing them together in the person of this charming little 'ash-grey pouched bear', as it is described by its Latin name.

Sharing our world with animals is a joy and a privilege – and a responsibility. It may have taken us thousands of years to become 'civilized'; it has taken many animal species millions of years to perfect their lifestyles and we have the ability to destroy them in a few decades. Ring-tailed lemurs (Fig 21) and bushbabies (Fig 22) together with hundreds of other species exist on a knife-edge. It is within our power to save them or consign them to history with the Tasmanian tiger and Mexican grizzly – the last of these magnificent bears hunted to extinction as late as 1967. Remember as you create your embroideries – whether of mouse or moose – it was their world before it was ours!

◀ *FIG 21*

Ring-tailed lemurs (Lemur catta) *are natives of the island of Madagascar where their habitat is slowly being eroded by man. This would make a lovely little study for anyone interested in conservation, either as a project or a gift. Frame simply, keeping attention on the main subject.*

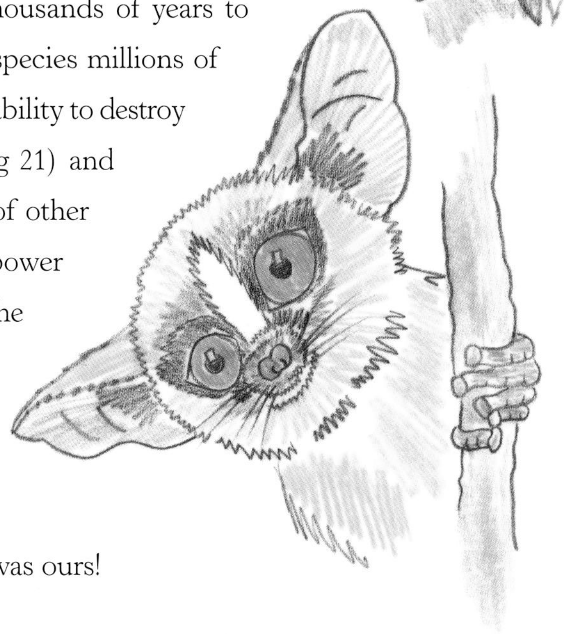

◀ *FIG 22*

The lesser bushbaby (Galago seneglensis) *is another creature dependent upon its own specialized environment of savannah, bush and woodland. No prizes for guessing where the inspiration for 'Gizmo' in the* Gremlins *films came from!*

KOALA AND EUCALYPT

Koalas are not, of course, bears but marsupials (they carry their young in pouches), though it is easy to see why the first European explorers made a mistake. In an age before the term 'teddy bear' was coined, these fellows could have been the prototype! Despite their cuddly appearance, however, they are quite capable of giving a nasty bite, or inflicting damage with those efficient, tree-climbing claws.

This study features broad fields of stitching, a limited palette of colours abutting and merging, separated by voiding and softened by the overlay of straight stitching – an exercise in radial *opus plumarium* on the grand scale. To complement and contrast with the chunky body of the koala, the eucalypt leaves are whippy and elegant, the branch elongated but sturdy enough to bear the weight of its burden.

TECHNIQUES

Stem stitch • Graduated stem stitch • Straight stitch

Shooting stitch • Radial *opus plumarium*

Directional *opus plumarium* • Seed stitch • Voiding

Subdued voiding • Surface couching

A design such as this could be elaborated with extra features relevant to its origin – Australian butterflies are colourful and dramatic and could be added to the study, either on a pale or dark background. Whilst the koala has no alternative foodstuff, wildflowers could soften the base of the design. For suggestions on working unfamiliar subject matter, see *Helen M. Stevens' World of Embroidery* (D&C 2002).

PLATE 30 ▶

Masterclass Five: Embroidery shown actual size 18.5 x 19.5cm (7¼ x 7¾in)

Trace off the template, including the position of the secondary cores. The 'fuzzy' contour is a useful reminder that the finished koala will be just a little larger than the given design, as softening the whole of the koala's outline will increase the size of that element of the picture. If working on a pale background (details 1 and 7) it is also an indication of which outlines should be worked in fragmented shadow lining.

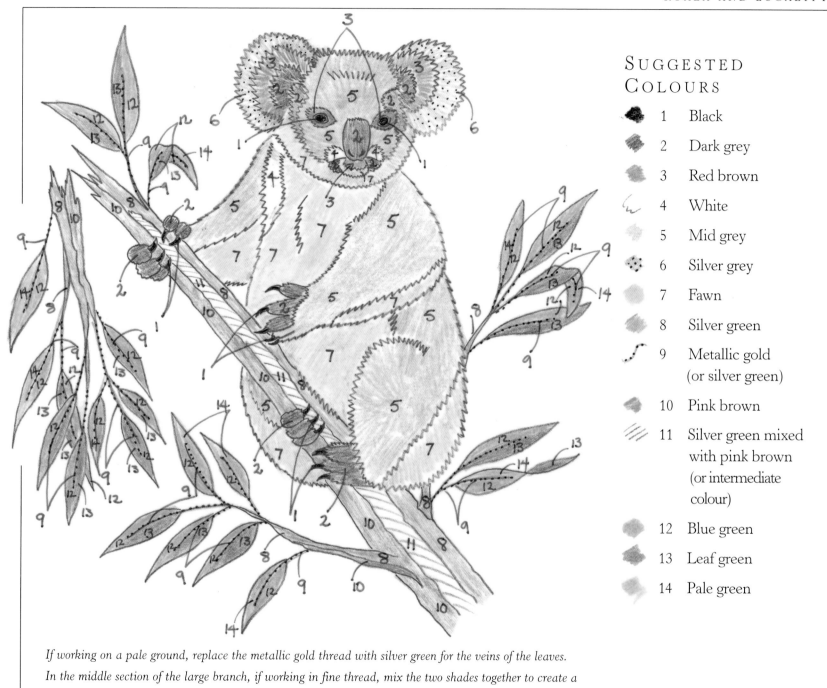

SUGGESTED COLOURS

	1	Black
	2	Dark grey
	3	Red brown
	4	White
	5	Mid grey
	6	Silver grey
	7	Fawn
	8	Silver green
	9	Metallic gold (or silver green)
	10	Pink brown
	11	Silver green mixed with pink brown (or intermediate colour)
	12	Blue green
	13	Leaf green
	14	Pale green

If working on a pale ground, replace the metallic gold thread with silver green for the veins of the leaves. In the middle section of the large branch, if working in fine thread, mix the two shades together to create a striated effect. Otherwise, choose an intermediate colour for this area. Alternatively, you could use either colour 8 or 10 for the base work, overlaying straight stitches in the other to give a similar feel. If possible, use a matt thread for the 'leathery' nose. I have created mid grey by mixing two shades.

DESIGN NOTES

Read through the design notes before you start stitching – the order of working is complex and important.

The imagined light source is diffuse (as though filtering through the leaf canopy above), but if working on a

pale background, shadow the lower elements of the design, keeping the fragmented shadowing well spaced.

BEGIN WITH THE KOALA . . .

Take a few moments to sort your threads; an extra very fine white or silver
thread would be useful to emphasize the outermost, fuzzy stratum.

1 If working on a pale background, shadow
line in black (1). Remember that the
radial work will feed into your fragmented lines,
so judge the angle of the stitches carefully. Use
a fine stem stitch to outline the nose and
nostrils and block in the pupils of the eyes in
upright straight stitching, also in black.
Continue on to shadow line the rest of the
koala's body, as appropriate.

2 Work three seed stitches (not shown on colour chart) in red brown (3) to create each nostril and block in the nose in upright straight stitching in dark grey (2). The large area of the nose now forms a diffuse central core. Towards its base, work precise strata of radial *opus plumarium* in red brown, white (4), dark grey and fawn (7).

Work an area of radial *opus plumarium* around each eye (angled towards the primary core) in red brown, and flood the main strata of radial work back towards the mid and upper nose in mid grey (5) and fawn.

Work the inside of the ear in strata of dark grey, red brown and silver grey (6) respectively, and begin to soften the ear with long white shooting stitches (right). Work both ears to this point and then continue the main flow of radial *opus plumarium* around the face and up to the ears, including a final short stratum in dark grey. Build up the softening effect with more straight shooting stitches in white and silver grey (left). Swing the stitches around to suggest the fuzziness of these ear 'whiskers'. If working on pale fabric, make sure your outer strata 'knit' with the fragmented outline. Highlight the eyes with white seed stitches.

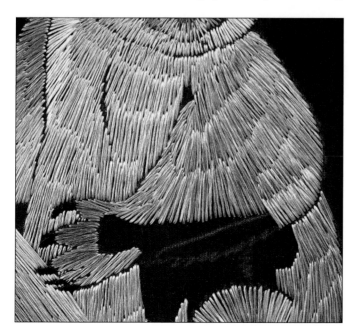

3 Begin to build up the multiple strata of the body in white, mid grey and fawn, working the foreleg towards a secondary core at the shoulder. Complete the near forepaw and toes in radial work in dark and mid grey and the claws in graduated stem stitch in black *before* working the surrounding areas. Void carefully between all the elements. Leave a voided line to suggest the sternum (a shadow line if working on a pale ground).

4 Continue down the body, working in substantial strata of radial work in mid grey and fawn, swinging around to create another secondary core at the haunch. Once the main body is complete go on to work the grasping feet and toes of the hindlegs before you work the branch (see detail 5), *then* soften the contours with straight stitching in the appropriate shades. Remember the softening effect must be added after any background elements (so the order of working this complex area is: main body, toes, claws, branch, softening effect).

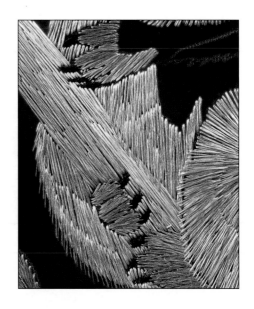

5 Work the far foreleg in radial *opus plumarium* in mid grey and fawn, the strata falling back towards a hidden diffuse core behind the animal's shoulder. Work the toes in dark grey and the claws in black, as before, and then begin work on the branch.

Working in fields of straight stitch lying along the length of the branch build up linear areas of colour in silver green (8), pink brown (10) and an intermediate shade appropriate to your choice of threads (11, see notes page 83). Complete the broken tip of the branch similarly in silver green and pink brown. Refer to Plate 25 and the colour chart for the larger of the two lower branches: work this in two strata of directional *opus plumarium*, sloping towards the lower edge of the branch. Leave a void where the lower branches emerge from the main branch.

NOW . . .

Go over the whole of your work, subduing and softening any voids and outlines that have not already been so treated. Refer to Plate 25 for stitch direction and the extent of the softening in various areas.

MOVING ON TO THE LEAVES . . .

6 Work the long whippy twigs in graduated stem stitch in silver grey. Work each leaf in directional *opus plumarium* in blue green (12), leaf green (13) and pale green (14), incorporating the opposite angle principle where appropriate (See Stitch Variations, page 93). Leave a void for the central vein. Infill the void with metallic gold thread (9), surface couched in a self-coloured shade.

7 If working on a pale background, shadow line carefully in black and then work the central veins in stem stitch in silver green. Build up both sides of all the leaves (including opposite angle work) in blue green, leaf green and pale green as indicated.

MATERIALS

FABRIC

The choice of fabric and threads can affect the ultimate appearance of any embroidery and, as with the choice of colourways, should be at the discretion of the embroiderer. However, to achieve satisfactory results, certain practical considerations need to be borne in mind.

For so-called flat-work embroidery which must be worked in a frame, it is essential that the fabric chosen for the background does not stretch. If the fabric stretches even slightly while the embroidery is in progress, when taken out of the frame it will contract to its normal size and the embroidery will be distorted. It is also a good idea to look for a smooth, evenweave fabric. Suitable fabrics include:

✳ Cotton
✳ Polyester cotton ('Percale')
✳ Linen

Pure silk may also be used, but avoid types with too much 'slub' in the weave as this will interrupt the flow of the embroidery stitches.

The embroideries in this book have been worked on an inexpensive cotton/polyester fabric (sometimes called 'Percale') which is very light-weight. Poly-cotton mixes (evenweave) in a heavier weight are also ideal for use in this type of embroidery. Larger pictures should be worked on heavier fabrics, small studies on light-

weights, but this rule can be adapted to the particular needs of the work in question.

When choosing fabric, try to avoid any fabrics which have too loose a weave, as this will result in too many stitches vying for space in too few threads of warp and weft. As a general rule, if the weave is open enough to be used for counted thread embroidery, it will be too wide for us!

THREADS

A variety of threads are necessary to achieve diverse effects but the ultimate choice of which type to use on a specific area is a personal one. Any thread suitable for 'flatwork' embroidery may be used for any of the techniques in this book. Natural fibres are easier to use than synthetics and include cotton, floss silk and twisted silk.

◀ *Pure silks and cottons are available in a glorious variety of colours and textures. Clockwise from bottom left: stranded cottons, stranded and twisted silks, Japanese floss silk, fine floss silk, spun (fine twisted) silk.*

✳ COTTON
Most embroiderers are familiar with stranded cotton. It is usually available in six-stranded skeins and strands should be used singly.

✳ FLOSS SILK
This is untwisted with a high sheen, and is also known as sleave or Japanese silk. It should be doubled or split (as appropriate to the type chosen) to match the gauge of a single strand of stranded cotton to complete most of the projects in this book.

✳ TWISTED SILK
This usually has several strands twisted together. Single strands of most twisted silks are approximately the same gauge as single strands of stranded cotton and should be used singly. Very fine details should be worked in finer gauges of thread if available.

✳ SYNTHETIC METALLIC THREADS
These are available in many formats in gold, silver and various other colours. The most versatile are several stranded threads which may be used entire where a thick gauge is required, or split into single strands for fine or delicate details.

'REAL' GOLD AND SILVER THREAD
These threads are usually made using a percentage of real gold or silver. Generally they comprise very narrow strips of leaf or fine metal twisted around a synthetic, cotton or silk core. 'Passing' thread is tightly wound and available in various gauges, the finest of which may be used directly in the needle, the thicker couched down. 'Jap' gold is more loosely wound, is also available in a variety of gauges, but is usually only suitable for couching.

BLENDING FILAMENTS
This term encompasses a vast number of specialist threads, but usually refers to threads which are made up of a number of strands of differing types, e.g. a silky thread together with a cellophane or sparkling thread. They may be used entire, or split down into their component parts which may be used separately.

TOOLS

Basic embroidery tools have remained unchanged for centuries and the essentials are described here.

EMBROIDERY FRAME
In flat embroidery the tension of the background fabric is all important (see Stitch Variations, page 92) and it is essential to work on an embroidery frame. Round, tambour hoops are best suited to fine embroidery as they produce an entirely uniform tension. Wooden hoops maintain their tension best. Always use a frame large enough to allow a generous amount of fabric around your design.

SCISSORS
You will need small scissors for threads, fine and sharp. I use pinking shears for cutting fabric, which also helps to prevent fraying. Don't use thread or fabric scissors to cut anything else or you will blunt the blades.

NEEDLES
These should always be chosen with the specific use of threads and fabrics in mind. 'Embroidery' needles are designed with a long eye and a sharp point. You will find a selection of sizes 5 to 10 are the most useful. Size 8 is ideal for use with a 'single strand' gauge as discussed above.

▼ Floss and twisted silk produce different effects: glossy, as shown on the plant and upper sides of the butterflies' wings, or with the subtler, matt glow illustrated by the underside of the wings. 10.75 x 12.75cm (4½ x 5in)

▲ Metallic and specialist materials. Clockwise from top left: imitation gold thread (stranded), real gold passing thread, coloured metallic threads, real silver passing thread, blending filaments, imitation silver thread (stranded) with bugle and seed beads.

▲ Working in stranded cotton and imitation metallic thread can create a soft, muted effect. 10 x 12.75cm (4 x 5in)

BASIC TECHNIQUES

Before you begin to embroider it is important to pay attention to the initial preparation and transfer of your design. Similarly, after your project is completed you need to give some thought to the presentation of the work.

TRANSFERRING A DESIGN

You will need (see picture above, left to right):
* Original design
* Tracing paper (use good quality 90gsm)
* 'H' pencil
* Drawing pins

* Dressmakers' carbon paper in a colour contrasting your fabric
* Fabric
* Tissue paper
* Tambour hoop

You will also need scissors and a smooth, hard surface on which to work. Ideally, this should be a wooden drawing board covered with several layers of lining paper.

1 Place the tracing paper over your design and carefully trace off the design, omitting any very fine details, e.g., whiskers, spiders' webs, butterflies' antennae. These lines, if transferred, could not be covered by single strands of thread and must be added freehand during the course of the embroidery.

2 Lay your fabric flat, and place the tracing on top of it. Pin the tracing in place with two drawing pins at the top right and left-hand corners. Interleave between fabric and tracing

with the carbon (colour side down) and hold secure with a third pin through the tracing at the bottom of the paper. Do not pin through the carbon.

With a firm, even pressure, re-draw each line of the design. After you have completed a few lines, carefully lift one corner of the tracing paper and carbon paper to check that your design is transferring successfully.

3 When the transfer is complete, remove the bottom drawing pin, lift back the tracing and remove the carbon paper. Check that every detail of the

design has been transferred before finally removing the tracing paper. You are now ready to mount your fabric, using tissue paper and a tambour hoop (see instructions opposite).

MOUNTING FABRIC IN A TAMBOUR HOOP

You will need:
* Fabric, with the design transferred
* Tissue paper
* Tambour hoop

1 Cut two sheets of tissue paper at least 5cm (2in) wider than the outer dimensions of your tambour hoop. Place the inner ring of your hoop on a flat surface and lay one sheet of tissue

paper over it. Lay your fabric over the tissue paper, and ensure that the design is centred in the ring. Lay a second sheet of tissue paper over the fabric and slip the outer ring of the hoop over the entire 'sandwich'. Tighten the screw until the fabric and paper is held firmly.

2 Trim the upper sheet of tissue paper inside and outside the upper ring (shown above). Turn the hoop over and trim the lower sheet of tissue paper similarly. The tissue paper will protect your fabric from abrasion by the hoop and keep the handled edges clean. You are now ready to begin your embroidery.

MOUNTING AND FRAMING YOUR WORK

You will need (see picture above):
* Backing board (rigid cardboard, foamboard or hardboard)
* Acid free cartridge paper (cut to the same size as the backing board)
* Lacing thread (a mercerised cotton is recommended)
* Two crewel needles (large enough to take your chosen cotton)
* Scissors

1 When your embroidery is complete press it on the wrong side, without steam (after checking the manufacturer's instructions for fabric and thread). Always press through another piece of fabric, and be *particularly* careful if you have used blending or other specialist filaments, especially cellophane threads.

It is essential to mount your work under similar tension to that exerted upon the fabric whilst in the tambour hoop. Lace it firmly onto a rigid backing board to achieve this tension. Make sure your backing board is large enough to take the whole design, with enough space at each edge to allow for framing.

2 Place the cartridge paper carefully between the board and the fabric. Next, position your embroidery, always making sure that the warp/weft of the fabric lies straight in relation the edges of the board.

3 Invert the ensemble so that the embroidery is face down, with the cartridge paper and board on top of it. Cut the fabric to size, allowing a comfortable overlap. Fold the two sides in toward the centre of the board. Cut a long but manageable piece of lacing thread and thread a needle at each end, leaving two 'tails', of similar length.

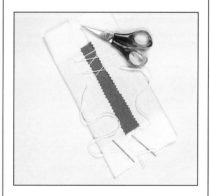

Working from the top, insert a needle on either side and lace the two sides of the fabric together, in corset fashion, until you reach the bottom. If you run out of thread simply tie the thread off and begin again.

4 Fold the top and bottom of the fabric toward the centre and repeat the lacing process. Always tie off the ends of the lacing thread with firm, non-slip knots and snip off any extra thread which is left. It takes a little

practise to achieve the perfect tension. Do not over tighten the laces as the thread may break, or rip the fabric, but do not be afraid to exert a reasonable pull on the work as only in this way will the original tension of the fabric on the tambour hoop be re-created.

5 The choice of framing is a personal matter, but always be prepared to take professional advice as the framing can make or mar a picture. A window mount is a good idea to keep the glass away from the fabric (and is essential if beads or thick specialist threads have been used) and remember that a frame should complement rather than dominate your design.

STITCH VARIATIONS

The stitches in this book are a combination of traditional embroidery stitches and contemporary innovations. They are flexible and adaptable: a single basic stitch such as stem stitch, depending on how it is applied, can produce a variety of effects, from a fine, sinuous line to a broad, strong one, with an infinite choice of widths, curves and reflexes within each variation.

The stitches fall into several distinct categories: linear, filling and decorative. Each has its own special properties and is suited to the description of certain shapes, fields and textures.

When working on a hoop the fabric *must* be taut within the frame. Stitches are always worked by the 'stab and pull' method. The needle is pushed through the fabric from above, the embroiderer's hand then moves to the back and pulls the needle through the fabric so the stitch forms smoothly on the surface. The next stitch is begun by pushing the needle up through the fabric from the reverse of the work, the hand brought to the front to pull the needle through, prior to beginning the routine once again.

LINEAR STITCHES

1 STEM STITCH
Always work from the top of any line to be described (on a natural history subject the outer extremity). Work *with* the curve of the subject: bring your needle out just to the outside of the curve and put it in on the inside of the curve.

a Fine/narrow stem stitch
Overlap the stitches by only a small proportion of the stitch length. The line created is only the width of a single stitch, creating a fine, sinuous effect.

b Broad stem stitch
Overlap the stitches so that half to three-quarters of each stitch lies beside its neighbour. The juxtaposition of several stitches creates a thick, strong effect.

c Graduating stem stitch
Begin with a fine stem stitch, increase it to a one-half ratio, then to three-quarters ratio within the same line creating the effect of a gradually thickening line (such as describes a growing stem – narrower at the tip, broader at the base).

d Coiling stem stitch
Begin with small stitches to describe the tight curve at the centre of the coil and gradually lengthen the stitches as the curve becomes gentler.

e Reflexing stem stitch
Beginning at the tip of the line, work the chosen variation a–c until the direction of the curve begins to change. Take one straight stitch through the preceding stitch, directly along the pattern line. Begin the stem stitch again, bringing the needle up on the new outside of the curve.

2 STRAIGHT STITCH
There are occasions when a completely straight line in the pattern can be described by a simple, straight stitch, or when a large field of the design must be filled smoothly with abutting straight stitches, such as in landscape work. The fabric must be taut within your frame to work this technique successfully.

a Vertical straight stitch (long)
Work this stitch from the top downward. Usually the stitches will be angled toward their base, such as in the case of simple grass effects. Ensure the stitch completely covers the transfer line.

b Horizontal straight stitch (long)
This stitch is used in blocks to suggest landscape effects. Work *toward* any abutting groups of stitches. To suggest a break in perspective, void (see 4 below) between abutting fields. To blend shades within a single field, stitch into the abutting field.

c Free straight stitch (long or short)
Fine details, such as whiskers, do not appear as transferred pattern lines (see Basic Techniques, page 90). These can be worked freehand in straight stitches angled to suit the particular needs of the subject matter. Work *away* from abutting groups of stitches.

3 SHADOW LINING
Establish the direction of the imagined light source within your picture. Each element of the design away from this light source will be shadow lined. Put a pin in the work, its tip pointing in the direction of the light source, to remind you of its origin.

a Smooth shadow lining
Work a fine, accurate stem stitch along the pattern line, just to its underside.

b Fragmented shadow lining
Where a line is too irregular to permit shadow lining by stem stitch, use straight stitches tailored to the length of the section of outline to be described.

4 VOIDING
Where two fields of a filling technique abut (see below), with or without a shadow line, suggesting that one element of the design overlaps another, a narrow line void of stitching should be left between the two. In practice, this forms on the transferred pattern line dividing the two elements. It should be approximately as wide as the gauge of thread used for the embroidery itself. To check that the width is correct, loosely position a strand of the thread along the 'valley' of the void. If it fits snugly, the width is correct.

FILLING STITCHES

1 OPUS PLUMARIUM
This literally means feather work and emulates the way in which feathers lie smoothly, yet with infinite changes of direction, upon a bird's body. The angle of the stitches sweeps around without breaking the flow of the stitching itself

and this in turn catches the light, refracting it back from the stitching and giving a three-dimensional impression.

a Radial opus plumarium (single or first stratum)

Begin with a stitch central to the field to be covered. This, and all subsequent stitches, are worked from the *outer* edge of the transferred pattern line *inwards* toward the centre of the motif. Bring the needle out immediately adjacent to the top of the first stitch. Slip the needle beneath the first stitch and through the fabric about two-thirds of the way down

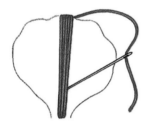

its length. This advances the angle of the stitching. Subsequent stitches can be either full length or shorter and angled as described, allowing the embroidery to fan out and cover the field without too many stitches 'bunching' at the inner core of the motif. A gradual advancement of the angle is achieved by working the angled stitches longer (e.g., three-quarters of the length of full stitches), more acute advancement of the angle by working them shorter (one quarter to half of the length of the full stitches).

b Radial opus plumarium (subsequent strata)

Where a broad field of stitches is

required to fill a motif, several strata of *opus plumarium* may be required.

Work the first stratum by the single stratum method described above. Always stitching *inwards* (toward the core of the motif), work the second stratum by taking a first stitch at the centre of the field. Stitch into the first stratum (do not leave a void) and, following the established flow of the stitching, fan out on either side of the first stitch, advancing the angle when necessary, as before. Subsequent strata are worked similarly.

c Directional opus plumarium (single or first stratum)

Where the core of the motif is elongated (such as the central vein of a simple elliptic leaf) the stitches should flow smoothly along its length. Again, always stitch inwards, bringing the needle out

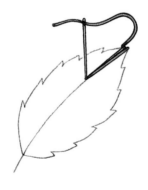

at the outer edge of the motif and in toward its centre.

Begin at the tip of the motif (or outer extremity of the first stratum) and take the first stitch inwards to abut the tip of the elongated core. Work your way down the field to be covered advancing the angle as necessary, as described above (a).

d Directional opus plumarium (subsequent strata)

Work the first strata as described above. Again working from the direction of the

tip of the motif inwards, create subsequent strata by stitching into the previous stratum (do not void), advancing the angle of the stitching as necessary to match the abutting stitches.

2 OPPOSITE ANGLE STITCHING

This is used to create the effect of reflex, e.g., where a leaf or petal curls forward or backward to reveal its underside.

Following the principles of *opus plumarium* work the stitches at an exactly opposite angle to the abutting field. (Occasionally the angles will be similar in actuality, but opposite in relation to the concept of the directional stitching.) Where necessary void between the two.

3 SNAKE STITCH

This is used to describe long, sinuous shapes, such as broad blades of grass or other linear leaves.

a Simple snake stitch

Begin at the tip of the motif, taking the first stitch in the direction of the curve to be described. For subsequent stitches, bring the needle out on the *outside* of

the curve and in on the *inside*. Work smoothly down the motif, advancing the angle of stitches, if necessary, by the *opus plumarium* method and lengthening the stitches where appropriate, as with graduating stem stitch (see above).

b Reflexing snake stitch

Begin at the point of reflex, where the direction of the curve changes. Firstly, take a stitch angled across the field slanting between the tip and base of the

curve. Work upwards to the tip, bringing the needle out on the outside of the curve and in on the inside until the upper field is complete. Advance the angle of stitching by the *opus plumarium* method if necessary. Complete the lower field by returning to the central stitch and working down the motif, again bringing the needle out on the outside and in on the inside of the curve. Advance the stitch angle as necessary.

4 DALMATIAN DOG TECHNIQUE

This is used to create a single, smooth field of embroidery where an area of one colour is completely encompassed by another colour. Used within *opus plumarium* (either radial or directional).

a Simple Dalmatian dog

Establish the radial or directional flow of the *opus plumarium*. Working the stitches at exactly the same angle as the main field of *opus plumarium* to follow,

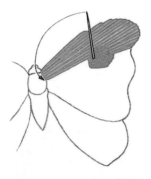

work the spots or other fields to be covered first. When completed, flood the rest of the *opus plumarium* around them, again paying careful attention to the flow of the stitches.

b Multiple Dalmatian dog

This technique can create a 'spot within a spot' or any other irregular pattern.

Establish either the radial or directional flow of the *opus plumarium*.

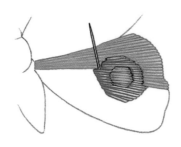

Maintaining the angle of stitching as above, work the innermost colour first, followed by outer field or fields of colour until the spots or other shapes are complete. Flood the surrounding *opus plumarium* around them.

DECORATIVE STITCHES

1 SEED STITCH

Fine, short, straight stitches worked directly onto the fabric, occasionally superimposed over other embroidery.

2 TICKING

These are seed stitches overlaying *opus plumarium*, worked at exactly the same angle as the underlying work but taken in the opposite direction, i.e., against the flow of the work.

3 STUDDING

These are seed stitches which overlay *opus plumarium*, but are worked at right angles to the underlying stitches.

4 SHOOTING STITCH

Long straight stitches taken in the opposite direction to the underlying radial or directional work.

5 CHEVRON STITCH

Two long straight stitches are angled to meet. Infill with a third straight stitch if necessary. To create a very sharp angle (such as a thistle spike) work a fourth straight stitch in a fine gauge of thread through the body of the motif.

6 DOTTING/SPECKLING

Work very short straight stitches, only as long as the width of the thread, to create an impression of tiny round dots. Work the stitches close together and in random directions.

7 FLOATING EMBROIDERY

This allows the threads to lie loosely on the fabric, falling into spontaneous shapes. Do not transfer the design to be formed onto the background fabric.

Take a long stitch from the inside to the outside of the motif, putting a finger or pencil under the thread to keep it away from the fabric. Take a very small stitch at the outer point of the motif to bring the thread back to the

surface. Take a third stitch back to the core of the motif, again keeping a finger beneath the thread. Repeat the process, removing the finger or pencil when several strands have built up.

8 SURFACE COUCHING

Usually a goldwork technique, this can be used effectively on various threads.

Bring the thread to be couched (the base thread) through the fabric to the surface of the work. If it is too thick to be brought through the fabric, lay it in place and hold it down with a thumb. Thread a second needle with a finer thread (the couching thread) and bring it up through the fabric immediately alongside the base thread. Take a tiny stitch over the base thread, at right angles to it, and repeat at regular intervals, effectively using the couching thread to whip the base thread into place along the transferred pattern line. Pay particular attention to whipping the beginning and the end of the base thread into place if it is lying wholly on the surface of the work.

9 SUBDUED VOIDING

Where two fields of *opus plumarium* abut and are separated by a voided line, the effect can be softened by working fine straight stitches, at the angle of the underlying work, across the void. Use a shade similar to that of the embroidered field 'closer' in perspective to the viewer, e.g., where a bird's wing lies over its body, or the angle of its neck creates a break in perspective. Work the overlying stitches at regular intervals, allowing the voided line to show through.

SUPPLIERS

There are many manufacturers and suppliers of embroidery materials and equipment and I have suggested a few here.
* This indicates suppliers who will accept orders direct from the given address via mail order.

Coats Crafts UK,
PO Box 22, The Lingfield Estate,
McMullen Road, Darlington,
Co. Durham DL1 1YQ, UK
tel: 01325 365457
Stranded cottons

Coats and Clark,
Consumer Services
PO Box 12229
Greenville, SC 29612-0229, USA
tel: (800) 648 1479
www.coatsandclark.com
Stranded cottons and fabrics

DMC Creative World Ltd.,
Pullman Road, Wigston,
Leicestershire LE18 2DY, UK
tel: 0116 281 1040
fax: 0116 281 3592
www.dmc/cw.com
*Stranded cotton, imitation
gold and silver threads*

DMC Corporation,
Building 10, Port Kearny,
South Kearny, NJ 07032, USA
tel: (US) 201 589 0606
*Stranded cotton, imitation gold
and silver threads*

Japanese Embroidery Centre UK,*
White Lodge, Littlewick Road,
Lower Knaphill, Woking,
Surrey GU21 2JU, UK
tel: 01483 476246
*Floss silk, real gold and silver threads,
imitation gold, silver and coloured
metallic threads*

Kreinik Manufacturing. Co., Inc.,
3106 Timanus Lane, Suite 101,
Baltimore, MD 21244, USA
tel: (US) 800 537 2166
(UK ++01325 365 457)
www.kreinik.com
email: kreinik@kreinik.com
*Silks, blending filaments and
metallic threads*

Madeira Threads (UK) Ltd.,
PO Box 6, Thirsk,
North Yorkshire YO7 3BX, UK
tel: 01845 524880
www.madeira.co.uk
email: acts@madeira
Twisted/stranded silks

Pearsall's,
Tancrad Street, Taunton,
Somerset TA1 1RY, UK
tel: 01823 274700
Shop online at
www.pearsallsembroidery.com
Stranded pure silk threads

Pipers Specialist Silks, *
Chinnerys, Egremont Street,
Glemsford, Sudbury,
Suffolk CI10 7SA, UK
tel: 01787 280920
www.pipers-silks.com
email: susanpeck@pipers-silks.com
*Floss and spun (twisted) silk. Exclusive silk
kits designed by Helen M. Stevens*

Stephen Simpson Ltd., *
50 Manchester Road,
Preston PR1 3YH, UK
tel: 01772 556688
Real gold and silver threads

The Voirrey Embroidery Centre, *
Brimstage Hall,
Wirral L63 6JA, UK
tel: 0151 3423514
General embroidery supplies

Helen M. Stevens
Lectures, masterclasses and themed
holidays are available based around
Helen's work. For full details of these
and other products and activities,
including masterclass lessons online,
visit: www.helenmstevens.co.uk

Alternatively, contact Helen via
David & Charles, Brunel House,
Forde Close, Newton Abbot, Devon,
TQ12 4PU, UK

ACKNOWLEDGMENTS

As ever, I am grateful to my support team for all their help in the preparation of this book (Cheryl Brown at David & Charles, Nigel and
Angela Salmon for photography and presentation, Lin Clements for editing and Pam my wonderful PA), and to family and friends for their
patience! I am also, of course, particularly grateful to all the animals, without whom it would not have been possible to create such a work
at all, especially certain cats and their owners who donated and collected whiskers. These include (cats only!) Adam, Roger, Chloe,
Brandy, Lucy, Tibbs and others, not forgetting Ragnar Hairybritches, My Favourite, Balthazaar, Bilko and his Mum,
Benson and Tess, who all appear by kind permission of their owners (or staff, in the case of the cats!).
Thank you, too, to those who have given permission for reproduction of certain colour plates: Plate 2 Lucy Horne;
4 Miss M. Joynson; 13 Clive and Linda Scott; 22 Joan Boughton; 24 Doreen Barber; Masterclass One detail 1 Carolyn Pearce;
detail 2 The Embroiderers' Guild of Western Australia.

INDEX